WORDS OF WISDOM

COMPILED BY
GEORGE M. WILSON

A Journey through Psalms and Proverbs

NEW LIVING
TRANSLATION

Tyndale House Publishers, Inc.
Wheaton, Illinois

Foreword

The late Senator Everett Dirksen of Illinois once told me that one could not help but draw great inspiration from the reading of the Psalms and the Proverbs. For many years I made it a practice to read five Psalms and a chapter of the book of Proverbs each day, aside from my other Bible reading and study, and it has been a great blessing to me.

By reading five Psalms and one chapter of Proverbs daily, you will be able to read them through each month. The Psalms will tell you how to get along with God, and the Proverbs will tell you how to get along with your fellowman. In Deuteronomy 6:5 we read, "Thou shalt love the Lord thy God with all thine heart, and with all thy soul, and with all thy might" (KJV). In Leviticus 19:18 we read, "Don't seek vengeance. Don't bear a grudge; but love your neighbor as yourself, for I am Jehovah" (TLB). Both of these great affirmations are underlined in the Psalms and Proverbs.

In this book you have a wonderful treat in store. May God bless you as you begin to live in its pages.

Billy Graham

Preface

In a way unmatched by any other literature, the book of Psalms draws us apart from the workaday life of man, brings us into the sanctuary, and directs us into precious communion with God. The Hebrew word for Psalms is *tehillim,* which in a general way means "poems of praise composed to be sung."

The book of Psalms really gives us a summary of both the Old and New Testaments. All the way through the book, and particularly in the Messianic psalms, we find the message of the Christ to come. Our risen Lord referred to the Psalms in his last message before ascending to his Father. "When I was with you before, I told you that everything written about me . . . in the Psalms must all come true" (Luke 24:44). In Colossians 3:16, the apostle Paul tells the believers, "Let the words of Christ, in all their richness, live in your hearts and make you wise. Use his words to teach and counsel each other. Sing psalms and hymns and spiritual songs to God with thankful hearts."

While the Psalms are all divinely inspired, they were composed at different times for different occasions, and have been put together rather independently of each other. King David was probably the author of most of the Psalms. In 2 Samuel 23:1 he is referred to as the "psalmist of Israel." One psalm (Psalm 90) was a prayer of Moses. Other psalms were written by Asaph, for in 2 Chronicles 29:30 Hezekiah ordered the Levites to "praise the Lord with the psalms of David and Asaph." The chronicler also calls Asaph a seer, or prophet.

David's genius is found in his poetry. His lyrics became the Psalter for the early church of God. No other book, perhaps, is as helpful to a Christian's devotional life as is the book of Psalms.

The Psalms are divided into five sections, also called books. Each section concludes with "Amen" or "Hallelujah." The first section ends with Psalm 41, the second with Psalm 72, the third with Psalm 89, the fourth with Psalm 106. We have purposely not made these divisions in this devotional edition for the convenience of the reader using them for inspiration in his or her daily devotions.

George M. Wilson

Psalm 1

¹ Oh, the joys of those
    who do not follow the advice of the wicked,
    or stand around with sinners,
    or join in with scoffers.
² But they delight in doing everything the
    LORD wants;
    day and night they think about His law.
³ They are like trees planted along the riverbank,
    bearing fruit each season without fail.
  Their leaves never wither,
    and in all they do, they prosper.

⁴ But this is not true of the wicked.
    They are like worthless chaff, scattered by
      the wind.
⁵ They will be condemned at the time of judgment.
  Sinners will have no place among the godly.

⁶ For the LORD watches over the path of the
      godly,
    but the path of the wicked leads to destruction.

Psalm 2

¹ Why do the nations rage?
     Why do the people waste their time with
          futile plans?
² The kings of the earth prepare for battle;
     the rulers plot together
   against the LORD
     and against His Anointed One.
³ "Let us break their chains," they cry,
     "and free ourselves from this slavery."

⁴ But the One who rules in heaven laughs.
     The Lord scoffs at them.
⁵ Then in anger He rebukes them,
     terrifying them with His fierce fury.
⁶ For the LORD declares, "I have placed My chosen king
          on the throne
     in Jerusalem, My holy city."

⁷ The king proclaims the LORD's decree:
   "The LORD said to Me, 'You are My Son.
     Today I have become Your Father.
⁸ Only ask, and I will give You the nations as Your
          inheritance,
     the ends of the earth as Your possession.
⁹ You will break them with an iron rod
     and smash them like clay pots.'"

¹⁰ Now then, you kings, act wisely!
　　Be warned, you rulers of the earth!
¹¹ Serve the LORD with reverent fear,
　　and rejoice with trembling.
¹² Submit to God's royal Son, or He will become angry,
　　and you will be destroyed in the midst of your
　　　　pursuits—
　　for His anger can flare up in an instant.

　　But what joy for all who find protection in Him!

Psalm 3

A psalm of David, regarding the time David fled from his son Absalom.

¹ O LORD, I have so many enemies;
　　so many are against me.
² So many are saying,
　　"God will never rescue him!"   *Interlude*

³ But You, O LORD, are a shield around me,
　　my glory, and the One who lifts my head high.
⁴ I cried out to the LORD,
　　and He answered me from His holy mountain.
　　　　　　　　　　　　　　　　　　　　　　　Interlude

⁵ I lay down and slept.
　　I woke up in safety,
　　for the LORD was watching over me.

⁶ I am not afraid of ten thousand enemies
    who surround me on every side.

⁷ Arise, O LORD!
    Rescue me, My God!
  Slap all my enemies in the face!
    Shatter the teeth of the wicked!

⁸ Victory comes from You, O LORD.
    May Your blessings rest on Your people.   *Interlude*

Psalm 4

For the choir director: A psalm of David, to be accompanied by stringed instruments.

¹ Answer me when I call,
    O God who declares me innocent.
  Take away my distress.
    Have mercy on me and hear my prayer.

² How long will you people ruin my reputation?
    How long will you make these groundless accusations?
    How long will you pursue lies?   *Interlude*

³ You can be sure of this:
    The LORD has set apart the godly for Himself.
    The LORD will answer when I call to Him.

⁴ Don't sin by letting anger gain control over you.
    Think about it overnight and remain silent.   *Interlude*
⁵ Offer proper sacrifices,
    and trust in the LORD.

⁶ Many people say, "Who will show us better times?"
    Let the smile of Your face shine on us, LORD.
⁷ You have given me greater joy
    than those who have abundant harvests of grain
        and wine.

⁸ I will lie down in peace and sleep,
    for You alone, O LORD, will keep me safe.

Psalm 5

For the choir director: A psalm of David, to be accompanied by the flute.

¹ O LORD, hear me as I pray;
    pay attention to my groaning.
² Listen to my cry for help, My King and My God,
    for I will never pray to anyone but You.
³ Listen to my voice in the morning, LORD.
    Each morning I bring my requests to You and wait
        expectantly.

⁴ O God, You take no pleasure in wickedness;
    You cannot tolerate the slightest sin.

⁵ Therefore, the proud will not be allowed to stand in
      Your presence,
    for You hate all who do evil.
⁶ You will destroy those who tell lies.
    The LORD detests murderers and deceivers.

⁷ Because of Your unfailing love, I can enter Your house;
    with deepest awe I will worship at Your Temple.
⁸ Lead me in the right path, O LORD,
    or my enemies will conquer me.
  Tell me clearly what to do,
    and show me which way to turn.

⁹ My enemies cannot speak one truthful word.
    Their deepest desire is to destroy others.
  Their talk is foul, like the stench from an open grave.
    Their speech is filled with flattery.
¹⁰ O God, declare them guilty.
    Let them be caught in their own traps.
  Drive them away because of their many sins,
    for they rebel against You.

¹¹ But let all who take refuge in You rejoice;
    let them sing joyful praises forever.
  Protect them,
    so all who love Your name may be filled with joy.
¹² For You bless the godly, O LORD,
    surrounding them with Your shield of love.

Proverbs 1

These are the proverbs of Solomon, David's son, king of Israel.

²The purpose of these proverbs is to teach people wisdom and discipline, and to help them understand wise sayings. ³Through these proverbs, people will receive instruction in discipline, good conduct, and doing what is right, just, and fair. ⁴These proverbs will make the simpleminded clever. They will give knowledge and purpose to young people.

⁵Let those who are wise listen to these proverbs and become even wiser. And let those who understand receive guidance ⁶by exploring the depth of meaning in these proverbs, parables, wise sayings, and riddles.

⁷Fear of the LORD is the beginning of knowledge. Only fools despise wisdom and discipline.

⁸Listen, my child, to what your father teaches you. Don't neglect your mother's teaching. ⁹What you learn from them will crown you with grace and clothe you with honor.

¹⁰My child, if sinners entice you, turn your back on them! ¹¹They may say, "Come and join us. Let's hide and kill someone! Let's ambush the innocent! ¹²Let's swallow them alive as the grave swallows its victims. Though they are in the prime of life, they will go down into the pit of death. ¹³And the loot we'll get! We'll fill our houses with all kinds of things! ¹⁴Come on, throw in your lot with us; we'll split our loot with you."

¹⁵Don't go along with them, my child! Stay far away from their paths. ¹⁶They rush to commit crimes. They hurry to commit murder. ¹⁷When a bird sees a trap being set, it stays away. ¹⁸But not these people! They set an ambush for themselves; they booby-trap their own lives! ¹⁹Such is the fate of all who are greedy for gain. It ends up robbing them of life.

²⁰Wisdom shouts in the streets. She cries out in the public square. ²¹She calls out to the crowds along the main street, and to those in front of city hall. ²²"You simpletons!" she cries. "How long will you go on being simpleminded? How long will you mockers relish your mocking? How long will you fools fight the facts? ²³Come here and listen to me! I'll pour out the spirit of wisdom upon you and make you wise.

²⁴"I called you so often, but you didn't come. I reached out to you, but you paid no attention. ²⁵You ignored my advice and rejected the correction I offered. ²⁶So I will laugh when you are in trouble! I will mock you when disaster overtakes you—²⁷when calamity overcomes you like a storm, when you are engulfed by trouble, and when anguish and distress overwhelm you.

²⁸"I will not answer when they cry for help. Even though they anxiously search for me, they will not find me. ²⁹For they hated knowledge and chose not to fear the LORD. ³⁰They rejected my advice and paid no attention when I corrected them. ³¹That is why they must eat the bitter fruit

of living their own way. They must experience the full
terror of the path they have chosen. [32]For they are simpletons who turn away from me—to death. They are fools,
and their own complacency will destroy them. [33]But all
who listen to me will live in peace and safety, unafraid of
harm."

Notes

_____

_____

_____

_____

_____

_____

_____

_____

_____

_____

_____

_____

_____

_____

_____

_____

_____

_____

_____

_____

_____

_____

_____

_____

_____

_____

_____

_____

_____

_____

Psalm 6

For the choir director: A psalm of David, to be accompanied by an eight-stringed instrument.

¹ O LORD, do not rebuke me in Your anger
  or discipline me in Your rage.
² Have compassion on me, LORD, for I am weak.
  Heal me, LORD, for my body is in agony.
³ I am sick at heart.
  How long, O LORD, until You restore me?

⁴ Return, O LORD, and rescue me.
  Save me because of Your unfailing love.
⁵ For in death, who remembers You?
  Who can praise You from the grave?

⁶ I am worn out from sobbing.
  Every night tears drench my bed;
  my pillow is wet from weeping.
⁷ My vision is blurred by grief;
  my eyes are worn out because of all my enemies.

⁸ Go away, all you who do evil,
  for the LORD has heard my crying.

⁹ The LORD has heard my plea;
　　the LORD will answer my prayer.
¹⁰ May all my enemies be disgraced and terrified.
　　May they suddenly turn back in shame.

Psalm 7

*A psalm of David, which he sang to the LORD concerning Cush of the tribe
of Benjamin.*

¹ I come to You for protection, O LORD My God.
　　Save me from my persecutors—rescue me!
² If You don't, they will maul me like a lion,
　　tearing me to pieces with no one to rescue me.

³ O LORD My God, if I have done wrong
　　or am guilty of injustice,
⁴ if I have betrayed a friend
　　or plundered my enemy without cause,
⁵ then let my enemies capture me.
　　Let them trample me into the ground.
　　Let my honor be left in the dust.　　　　　　*Interlude*

⁶ Arise, O LORD, in anger!
　　Stand up against the fury of my enemies!
　　Wake up, My God, and bring justice!
⁷ Gather the nations before You.
　　Sit on Your throne high above them.

⁸ The LORD passes judgment on the nations.
  Declare me righteous, O LORD,
  for I am innocent, O Most High!
⁹ End the wickedness of the ungodly,
  but help all those who obey You.
For You look deep within the mind and heart,
  O righteous God.

¹⁰ God is my shield,
  saving those whose hearts are true and right.
¹¹ God is a judge who is perfectly fair.
  He is angry with the wicked every day.

¹² If a person does not repent,
  God will sharpen His sword;
  he will bend and string His bow.
¹³ He will prepare His deadly weapons
  and ignite His flaming arrows.

¹⁴ The wicked conceive evil;
  they are pregnant with trouble
  and give birth to lies.
¹⁵ They dig a pit to trap others
  and then fall into it themselves.
¹⁶ They make trouble,
  but it backfires on them.
They plan violence for others,
  but it falls on their own heads.

¹⁷ I will thank the LORD because He is just;
      I will sing praise to the name of the LORD Most High.

Psalm 8

For the choir director: A psalm of David, to be accompanied by a
stringed instrument.

¹ O LORD, our Lord, the majesty of Your name fills the
      earth!
      Your glory is higher than the heavens.

² You have taught children and nursing infants
      to give You praise.
  They silence Your enemies
      who were seeking revenge.

³ When I look at the night sky and see the work of Your
      fingers—
      the moon and the stars You have set in place—
⁴ what are mortals that You should think of us,
      mere humans that You should care for us?
⁵ For You made us only a little lower than God,
      and You crowned us with glory and honor.
⁶ You put us in charge of everything You made,
      giving us authority over all things—
⁷ the sheep and the cattle
      and all the wild animals,

⁸ the birds in the sky, the fish in the sea,
  and everything that swims the ocean currents.

⁹ O LORD, our Lord, the majesty of Your name fills the
  earth!

Psalm 9

For the choir director: A psalm of David, to be sung to the tune "Death of the Son."

¹ I will thank You, LORD, with all my heart;
  I will tell of all the marvelous things You have done.
² I will be filled with joy because of You.
  I will sing praises to Your name, O Most High.

³ My enemies turn away in retreat;
  they are overthrown and destroyed before You.
⁴ For You have judged in my favor;
  from Your throne, You have judged with fairness.

⁵ You have rebuked the nations and destroyed the
    wicked;
  You have wiped out their names forever.
⁶ My enemies have met their doom;
  their cities are perpetual ruins.
  Even the memory of their uprooted cities is lost.

⁷ But the LORD reigns forever,
  executing judgment from His throne.

⁸ He will judge the world with justice
    and rule the nations with fairness.

⁹ The LORD is a shelter for the oppressed,
    a refuge in times of trouble.
¹⁰ Those who know Your name trust in You,
    for You, O LORD, have never abandoned anyone who
        searches for You.

¹¹ Sing praises to the LORD who reigns in Jerusalem.
    Tell the world about His unforgettable deeds.
¹² For He who avenges murder cares for the helpless.
    He does not ignore those who cry to Him for help.

¹³ LORD, have mercy on me.
    See how I suffer at the hands of those who hate me.
    Snatch me back from the jaws of death.
¹⁴ Save me, so I can praise You publicly at Jerusalem's
        gates,
    so I can rejoice that You have rescued me.

¹⁵ The nations have fallen into the pit they dug for others.
    They have been caught in their own trap.
¹⁶ The LORD is known for His justice.
    The wicked have trapped themselves in their own
        snares.   *Quiet Interlude*

¹⁷ The wicked will go down to the grave.
    This is the fate of all the nations who ignore God.

¹⁸ For the needy will not be forgotten forever;
     the hopes of the poor will not always be
       crushed.

¹⁹ Arise, O LORD!
     Do not let mere mortals defy You!
     Let the nations be judged in Your presence!
²⁰ Make them tremble in fear, O LORD.
     Let them know they are merely human.   *Interlude*

Psalm 10

¹ O LORD, why do You stand so far away?
     Why do You hide when I need You the most?
² Proud and wicked people viciously oppress the poor.
     Let them be caught in the evil they plan for others.
³ For they brag about their evil desires;
     they praise the greedy and curse the LORD.
⁴ These wicked people are too proud to seek God.
     They seem to think that God is dead.
⁵ Yet they succeed in everything they do.
     They do not see Your punishment awaiting them.
     They pour scorn on all their enemies.
⁶ They say to themselves, "Nothing bad will ever happen
       to us!
     We will be free of trouble forever!"

⁷ Their mouths are full of cursing, lies, and threats.
   Trouble and evil are on the tips of their tongues.
⁸ They lurk in dark alleys,
   murdering the innocent who pass by.

They are always searching
   for some helpless victim.
⁹ Like lions they crouch silently,
   waiting to pounce on the helpless.
Like hunters they capture their victims
   and drag them away in nets.
¹⁰ The helpless are overwhelmed and collapse;
   they fall beneath the strength of the wicked.
¹¹ The wicked say to themselves, "God isn't
        watching!
   He will never notice!"

¹² Arise, O LORD!
   Punish the wicked, O God!
   Do not forget the helpless!
¹³ Why do the wicked get away with cursing God?
   How can they think, "God will never call us to
        account"?

¹⁴ But You do see the trouble and grief they cause.
   You take note of it and punish them.
The helpless put their trust in You.
   You are the defender of orphans.

¹⁵ Break the arms of these wicked, evil people!
     Go after them until the last one is destroyed!
¹⁶ The LORD is king forever and ever!
     Let those who worship other gods be swept from the
        land.

¹⁷ LORD, You know the hopes of the helpless.
     Surely You will listen to their cries and comfort them.
¹⁸ You will bring justice to the orphans and the oppressed,
     so people can no longer terrify them.

Proverbs 2

My child, listen to me and treasure my instructions. ²Tune your ears to wisdom, and concentrate on understanding. ³Cry out for insight and understanding. ⁴Search for them as you would for lost money or hidden treasure. ⁵Then you will understand what it means to fear the LORD, and you will gain knowledge of God. ⁶For the LORD grants wisdom! From His mouth come knowledge and understanding. ⁷He grants a treasure of good sense to the godly. He is their shield, protecting those who walk with integrity. ⁸He guards the paths of justice and protects those who are faithful to Him.

⁹Then you will understand what is right, just, and fair, and you will know how to find the right course of action

every time. [10]For wisdom will enter your heart, and knowledge will fill you with joy. [11]Wise planning will watch over you. Understanding will keep you safe.

[12]Wisdom will save you from evil people, from those whose speech is corrupt. [13]These people turn from right ways to walk down dark and evil paths. [14]They rejoice in doing wrong, and they enjoy evil as it turns things upside down. [15]What they do is crooked, and their ways are wrong.

[16]Wisdom will save you from the immoral woman, from the flattery of the adulterous woman. [17]She has abandoned her husband and ignores the covenant she made before God. [18]Entering her house leads to death; it is the road to hell. [19]The man who visits her is doomed. He will never reach the paths of life.

[20]Follow the steps of good men instead, and stay on the paths of the righteous. [21]For only the upright will live in the land, and those who have integrity will remain in it. [22]But the wicked will be removed from the land, and the treacherous will be destroyed.

Notes

Notes

Psalm 11

For the choir director: A psalm of David.

¹ I trust in the LORD for protection.
　　So why do you say to me,
　"Fly to the mountains for safety!
²　　The wicked are stringing their bows
　　　and setting their arrows in the bowstrings.
　　　They shoot from the shadows at those who do right.
³ The foundations of law and order have collapsed.
　　What can the righteous do?"

⁴ But the LORD is in His holy Temple;
　　the LORD still rules from heaven.
　He watches everything closely,
　　examining everyone on earth.
⁵ The LORD examines both the righteous and the wicked.
　　He hates everyone who loves violence.
⁶ He rains down blazing coals on the wicked,
　　punishing them with burning sulfur and scorching
　　　winds.
⁷ For the LORD is righteous, and He loves justice.
　　Those who do what is right will see His face.

Psalm 12

For the choir director: A psalm of David, to be accompanied by an eight-stringed instrument.

¹ Help, O LORD, for the godly are fast disappearing!
    The faithful have vanished from the earth!
² Neighbors lie to each other,
    speaking with flattering lips and insincere
        hearts.
³ May the LORD bring their flattery to an end
    and silence their proud tongues.
⁴ They say, "We will lie to our hearts' content.
    Our lips are our own—who can stop us?"

⁵ The LORD replies, "I have seen violence done to the
        helpless,
    and I have heard the groans of the poor.
  Now I will rise up to rescue them,
    as they have longed for me to do."
⁶ The LORD's promises are pure,
    like silver refined in a furnace,
        purified seven times over.

⁷ Therefore, LORD, we know You will protect the
        oppressed,
    preserving them forever from this lying generation,
⁸ even though the wicked strut about,
    and evil is praised throughout the land.

Psalm 13

For the choir director: A psalm of David.

¹ O Lord, how long will You forget me? Forever?
   How long will You look the other way?
² How long must I struggle with anguish in my soul,
   with sorrow in my heart every day?
   How long will my enemy have the upper hand?

³ Turn and answer me, O Lord My God!
   Restore the light to my eyes, or I will die.
⁴ Don't let my enemies gloat, saying, "We have defeated
   him!"
   Don't let them rejoice at my downfall.

⁵ But I trust in Your unfailing love.
   I will rejoice because You have rescued me.
⁶ I will sing to the Lord
   because He has been so good to me.

Psalm 14

For the choir director: A psalm of David.

¹ Only fools say in their hearts,
   "There is no God."
   They are corrupt, and their actions are evil;
   no one does good!

[2] The LORD looks down from heaven
    on the entire human race;
He looks to see if there is even one with real understanding,
    one who seeks for God.
[3] But no, all have turned away from God;
    all have become corrupt.
No one does good,
    not even one!

[4] Will those who do evil never learn?
    They eat up my people like bread;
    they wouldn't think of praying to the LORD.
[5] Terror will grip them,
    for God is with those who obey Him.
[6] The wicked frustrate the plans of the oppressed,
    but the LORD will protect His people.

[7] Oh, that salvation would come from Mount Zion to
    rescue Israel!
For when the LORD restores His people,
    Jacob will shout with joy, and Israel will rejoice.

Psalm 15

A psalm of David.

[1] Who may worship in Your sanctuary, LORD?
    Who may enter Your presence on Your holy hill?

²Those who lead blameless lives
  and do what is right,
  speaking the truth from sincere hearts.
³Those who refuse to slander others
  or harm their neighbors
  or speak evil of their friends.
⁴Those who despise persistent sinners,
  and honor the faithful followers of the LORD
  and keep their promises even when it hurts.
⁵Those who do not charge interest on the money they lend,
  and who refuse to accept bribes to testify against the
    innocent.

Such people will stand firm forever.

Proverbs 3

My child, never forget the things I have taught you. Store
my commands in your heart, ²for they will give you a long
and satisfying life. ³Never let loyalty and kindness get away
from you! Wear them like a necklace; write them deep
within your heart. ⁴Then you will find favor with both
God and people, and you will gain a good reputation.

⁵Trust in the LORD with all your heart; do not depend
on your own understanding. ⁶Seek His will in all you do,
and He will direct your paths.

⁷Don't be impressed with your own wisdom. Instead, fear the LORD and turn your back on evil. ⁸Then you will gain renewed health and vitality.

⁹Honor the LORD with your wealth and with the best part of everything your land produces. ¹⁰Then He will fill your barns with grain, and your vats will overflow with the finest wine.

¹¹My child, don't ignore it when the LORD disciplines you, and don't be discouraged when He corrects you. ¹²For the LORD corrects those He loves, just as a father corrects a child in whom he delights.

¹³Happy is the person who finds wisdom and gains understanding. ¹⁴For the profit of wisdom is better than silver, and her wages are better than gold. ¹⁵Wisdom is more precious than rubies; nothing you desire can compare with her. ¹⁶She offers you life in her right hand, and riches and honor in her left. ¹⁷She will guide you down delightful paths; all her ways are satisfying. ¹⁸Wisdom is a tree of life to those who embrace her; happy are those who hold her tightly.

¹⁹By wisdom the LORD founded the earth; by understanding He established the heavens. ²⁰By His knowledge the deep fountains of the earth burst forth, and the clouds poured down rain.

²¹My child, don't lose sight of good planning and insight. Hang on to them, ²²for they fill you with life and bring you honor and respect. ²³They keep you safe on your way and

keep your feet from stumbling. [24]You can lie down without fear and enjoy pleasant dreams. [25]You need not be afraid of disaster or the destruction that comes upon the wicked, [26]for the LORD is your security. He will keep your foot from being caught in a trap.

[27]Do not withhold good from those who deserve it when it's in your power to help them. [28]If you can help your neighbor now, don't say, "Come back tomorrow, and then I'll help you."

[29]Do not plot against your neighbors, for they trust you. [30]Don't make accusations against someone who hasn't wronged you.

[31]Do not envy violent people; don't copy their ways. [32]Such wicked people are an abomination to the LORD, but He offers His friendship to the godly.

[33]The curse of the LORD is on the house of the wicked, but His blessing is on the home of the upright.

[34]The LORD mocks at mockers, but He shows favor to the humble.

[35]The wise inherit honor, but fools are put to shame!

Notes

Psalm 16

A psalm of David.

¹ Keep me safe, O God,
　　for I have come to You for refuge.

² I said to the LORD, "You are my Master!
　　All the good things I have are from You."
³ The godly people in the land
　　are my true heroes!
　　I take pleasure in them!
⁴ Those who chase after other gods will be filled with
　　　sorrow.
　　I will not take part in their sacrifices
　　or even speak the names of their gods.

⁵ LORD, You alone are my inheritance, my cup of blessing.
　　You guard all that is mine.
⁶ The land You have given me is a pleasant land.
　　What a wonderful inheritance!

⁷ I will bless the LORD who guides me;
　　even at night my heart instructs me.
⁸ I know the LORD is always with me.
　　I will not be shaken, for He is right beside me.

⁹ No wonder my heart is filled with joy,
    and my mouth shouts His praises!
    My body rests in safety.
¹⁰ For You will not leave my soul among the dead
    or allow Your Godly One to rot in the grave.
¹¹ You will show me the way of life,
    granting me the joy of Your presence
    and the pleasures of living with You forever.

Psalm 17

A prayer of David.

¹ O LORD, hear my plea for justice.
    Listen to my cry for help.
  Pay attention to my prayer,
    for it comes from an honest heart.
² Declare me innocent,
    for You know those who do right.

³ You have tested my thoughts and examined my heart in
      the night.
    You have scrutinized me and found nothing amiss,
    for I am determined not to sin in what I say.
⁴ I have followed Your commands,
    which have kept me from going along with cruel and
      evil people.

⁵ My steps have stayed on Your path;
   I have not wavered from following You.

⁶ I am praying to You because I know You will answer,
      O God.
   Bend down and listen as I pray.
⁷ Show me Your unfailing love in wonderful ways.
   You save with Your strength
   those who seek refuge from their enemies.
⁸ Guard me as the apple of Your eye.
   Hide me in the shadow of Your wings.
⁹ Protect me from wicked people who attack me,
   from murderous enemies who surround me.

¹⁰ They are without pity.
   Listen to their boasting.
¹¹ They track me down, surround me,
   and throw me to the ground.
¹² They are like hungry lions, eager to tear me apart—
   like young lions in hiding, waiting for their
      chance.

¹³ Arise, O LORD!
   Stand against them and bring them to their knees!
   Rescue me from the wicked with Your sword!
¹⁴ Save me by Your mighty hand, O LORD,
   from those whose only concern is earthly gain.
   May they have their punishment in full.

May their children inherit more of the same,
and may the judgment continue to their children's
children.

¹⁵ But because I have done what is right, I will see You.
When I awake, I will be fully satisfied,
for I will see You face to face.

Psalm 18

*For the choir director: A psalm of David, the servant of the LORD. He sang this
song to the LORD on the day the LORD rescued him from all his enemies and
from Saul.*

¹ I love You, LORD; You are my strength.
² The LORD is my rock, my fortress, and my savior;
my God is my rock, in whom I find protection.
He is my shield, the strength of my salvation, and my
stronghold.
³ I will call on the LORD, who is worthy of praise,
for He saves me from my enemies.

⁴ The ropes of death surrounded me;
the floods of destruction swept over me.
⁵ The grave wrapped its ropes around me;
death itself stared me in the face.
⁶ But in my distress I cried out to the LORD;
yes, I prayed to my God for help.

He heard me from His sanctuary;
    my cry reached His ears.

7 Then the earth quaked and trembled;
    the foundations of the mountains shook;
    they quaked because of His anger.
8 Smoke poured from His nostrils;
    fierce flames leaped from His mouth;
    glowing coals flamed forth from Him.
9 He opened the heavens and came down;
    dark storm clouds were beneath His feet.
10 Mounted on a mighty angel, He flew,
    soaring on the wings of the wind.
11 He shrouded Himself in darkness,
    veiling His approach with dense rain clouds.
12 The brilliance of His presence broke through the clouds,
    raining down hail and burning coals.
13 The LORD thundered from heaven;
    the Most High gave a mighty shout.
14 He shot His arrows and scattered His enemies;
    His lightning flashed, and they were greatly confused.
15 Then at Your command, O LORD,
    at the blast of Your breath,
  the bottom of the sea could be seen,
    and the foundations of the earth were laid bare.

16 He reached down from heaven and rescued me;
    He drew me out of deep waters.

¹⁷ He delivered me from my powerful enemies,
    from those who hated me and were too strong for me.
¹⁸ They attacked me at a moment when I was weakest,
    but the LORD upheld me.
¹⁹ He led me to a place of safety;
    He rescued me because He delights in me.
²⁰ The LORD rewarded me for doing right;
    He compensated me because of my innocence.
²¹ For I have kept the ways of the LORD;
    I have not turned from my God to follow evil.
²² For all His laws are constantly before me;
    I have never abandoned His principles.
²³ I am blameless before God;
    I have kept myself from sin.
²⁴ The LORD rewarded me for doing right,
    because of the innocence of my hands in His sight.

²⁵ To the faithful You show Yourself faithful;
    to those with integrity You show integrity.
²⁶ To the pure You show Yourself pure,
    but to the wicked You show Yourself hostile.
²⁷ You rescue those who are humble,
    but You humiliate the proud.
²⁸ LORD, You have brought light to my life;
    my God, You light up my darkness.
²⁹ In Your strength I can crush an army;
    with my God I can scale any wall.

³⁰ As for God, His way is perfect.
  All the LORD's promises prove true.
  He is a shield for all who look to Him for
    protection.
³¹ For who is God except the LORD?
  Who but our God is a solid rock?
³² God arms me with strength;
  He has made my way safe.
³³ He makes me as surefooted as a deer,
  leading me safely along the mountain heights.
³⁴ He prepares me for battle;
  He strengthens me to draw a bow of
    bronze.
³⁵ You have given me the shield of Your salvation.
  Your right hand supports me;
  Your gentleness has made me great.
³⁶ You have made a wide path for my feet
  to keep them from slipping.

³⁷ I chased my enemies and caught them;
  I did not stop until they were conquered.
³⁸ I struck them down so they could not get up;
  they fell beneath my feet.
³⁹ You have armed me with strength for the battle;
  You have subdued my enemies under my feet.
⁴⁰ You made them turn and run;
  I have destroyed all who hated me.

41 They called for help, but no one came to rescue them.
    They cried to the LORD, but He refused to answer
        them.
42 I ground them as fine as dust carried by the wind.
    I swept them into the gutter like dirt.

43 You gave me victory over my accusers.
    You appointed me as the ruler over nations;
    people I don't even know now serve me.
44 As soon as they hear of me, they submit;
    foreigners cringe before me.
45 They all lose their courage
    and come trembling from their strongholds.

46 The LORD lives! Blessed be my rock!
    May the God of my salvation be exalted!
47 He is the God who pays back those who harm me;
    He subdues the nations under me
48   and rescues me from my enemies.
  You hold me safe beyond the reach of my
        enemies;
    You save me from violent opponents.
49 For this, O LORD, I will praise You among the
        nations;
    I will sing joyfully to Your name.
50 You give great victories to Your king;
    You show unfailing love to Your anointed,
    to David and all his descendants forever.

Psalm 19

For the choir director: A psalm of David.

¹ The heavens tell of the glory of God.
   The skies display His marvelous
      craftsmanship.
² Day after day they continue to speak;
   night after night they make Him known.
³ They speak without a sound or a word;
   their voice is silent in the skies;
⁴ yet their message has gone out to all the
      earth,
   and their words to all the world.

  The sun lives in the heavens
     where God placed it.
⁵ It bursts forth like a radiant bridegroom
   after his wedding.
  It rejoices like a great athlete
     eager to run the race.
⁶ The sun rises at one end of the heavens
   and follows its course to the other end.
   Nothing can hide from its heat.

⁷ The law of the LORD is perfect,
   reviving the soul.
  The decrees of the LORD are trustworthy,
     making wise the simple.

⁸ The commandments of the LORD are
   right,
   bringing joy to the heart.
   The commands of the LORD are clear,
   giving insight to life.
⁹ Reverence for the LORD is pure,
   lasting forever.
   The laws of the LORD are true;
   each one is fair.
¹⁰ They are more desirable than gold,
   even the finest gold.
   They are sweeter than honey,
   even honey dripping from the comb.
¹¹ They are a warning to those who hear
   them;
   there is great reward for those who obey them.

¹² How can I know all the sins lurking in my heart?
   Cleanse me from these hidden faults.
¹³ Keep me from deliberate sins!
   Don't let them control me.
   Then I will be free of guilt
   and innocent of great sin.

¹⁴ May the words of my mouth and the thoughts of
   my heart
   be pleasing to You,
   O LORD, my rock and my redeemer.

Psalm 20

For the choir director: A psalm of David.

¹ In times of trouble, may the LORD respond to
    your cry.
  May the God of Israel keep you safe from all
    harm.
² May He send you help from His sanctuary
    and strengthen you from Jerusalem.
³ May He remember all your gifts
    and look favorably on your burnt offerings.   *Interlude*

⁴ May He grant your heart's desire
    and fulfill all your plans.
⁵ May we shout for joy when we hear of your victory,
    flying banners to honor our God.
  May the LORD answer all your prayers.

⁶ Now I know that the LORD saves His anointed king.
    He will answer him from His holy heaven
    and rescue him by His great power.
⁷ Some nations boast of their armies and weapons,
    but we boast in the LORD our God.
⁸ Those nations will fall down and collapse,
    but we will rise up and stand firm.

⁹ Give victory to our king, O LORD!
    Respond to our cry for help.

Proverbs 4

My children, listen to me. Listen to your father's instruction. Pay attention and grow wise, [2]for I am giving you good guidance. Don't turn away from my teaching. [3]For I, too, was once my father's son, tenderly loved by my mother as an only child.

[4]My father told me, "Take my words to heart. Follow my instructions and you will live. [5]Learn to be wise, and develop good judgment. Don't forget or turn away from my words. [6]Don't turn your back on wisdom, for she will protect you. Love her, and she will guard you. [7]Getting wisdom is the most important thing you can do! And whatever else you do, get good judgment. [8]If you prize wisdom, she will exalt you. Embrace her and she will honor you. [9]She will place a lovely wreath on your head; she will present you with a beautiful crown."

[10]My child, listen to me and do as I say, and you will have a long, good life. [11]I will teach you wisdom's ways and lead you in straight paths. [12]If you live a life guided by wisdom, you won't limp or stumble as you run. [13]Carry out my instructions; don't forsake them. Guard them, for they will lead you to a fulfilled life.

[14]Do not do as the wicked do or follow the path of evildoers. [15]Avoid their haunts. Turn away and go somewhere else, [16]for evil people cannot sleep until they have done their evil deed for the day. They cannot rest unless they have

caused someone to stumble. [17]They eat wickedness and drink violence!

[18]The way of the righteous is like the first gleam of dawn, which shines ever brighter until the full light of day. [19]But the way of the wicked is like complete darkness. Those who follow it have no idea what they are stumbling over.

[20]Pay attention, my child, to what I say. Listen carefully. [21]Don't lose sight of my words. Let them penetrate deep within your heart, [22]for they bring life and radiant health to anyone who discovers their meaning.

[23]Above all else, guard your heart, for it affects everything you do.

[24]Avoid all perverse talk; stay far from corrupt speech.

[25]Look straight ahead, and fix your eyes on what lies before you. [26]Mark out a straight path for your feet; then stick to the path and stay safe. [27]Don't get sidetracked; keep your feet from following evil.

Notes

Psalm 21

For the choir director: A psalm of David.

¹ How the king rejoices in Your strength, O LORD!
   He shouts with joy because of Your victory.
² For You have given him his heart's desire;
   You have held back nothing that he requested.

Interlude

³ You welcomed him back with success and
   prosperity.
   You placed a crown of finest gold on his head.
⁴ He asked You to preserve his life,
   and You have granted his request.
   The days of his life stretch on forever.
⁵ Your victory brings him great honor,
   and You have clothed him with splendor and
   majesty.
⁶ You have endowed him with eternal blessings.
   You have given him the joy of being in Your presence.
⁷ For the king trusts in the LORD.
   The unfailing love of the Most High will keep him
   from stumbling.

⁸ You will capture all Your enemies.
    Your strong right hand will seize all those who hate
        You.
⁹ You will destroy them as in a flaming furnace
    when You appear.
  The LORD will consume them in His anger;
    fire will devour them.
¹⁰ You will wipe their children from the face of the earth;
    they will never have descendants.
¹¹ Although they plot against You,
    their evil schemes will never succeed.
¹² For they will turn and run
    when they see Your arrows aimed at them.

¹³ We praise You, LORD, for all Your glorious power.
    With music and singing we celebrate Your mighty acts.

Psalm 22

For the choir director: A psalm of David, to be sung to the tune
"Doe of the Dawn."

¹ My God, My God! Why have You forsaken Me?
    Why do You remain so distant?
    Why do You ignore My cries for help?
² Every day I call to You, My God, but You do not answer.
    Every night You hear My voice, but I find no relief.

³ Yet You are holy.
    The praises of Israel surround Your throne.
⁴ Our ancestors trusted in You,
    and You rescued them.
⁵ You heard their cries for help and saved them.
    They put their trust in You and were never disappointed.

⁶ But I am a worm and not a man.
    I am scorned and despised by all!
⁷ Everyone who sees Me mocks Me.
    They sneer and shake their heads, saying,
⁸ "Is this the One who relies on the LORD?
    Then let the LORD save Him!
 If the LORD loves Him so much,
    let the LORD rescue Him!"

⁹ Yet You brought Me safely from My mother's womb
    and led Me to trust You when I was a nursing infant.
¹⁰ I was thrust upon You at My birth.
    You have been My God from the moment I was born.

¹¹ Do not stay so far from Me,
    for trouble is near,
    and no one else can help Me.
¹² My enemies surround Me like a herd of bulls;
    fierce bulls of Bashan have hemmed Me in!
¹³ Like roaring lions attacking their prey,
    they come at Me with open mouths.

¹⁴ My life is poured out like water,
    and all My bones are out of joint.
  My heart is like wax,
    melting within Me.
¹⁵ My strength has dried up like sunbaked clay.
    My tongue sticks to the roof of My mouth.
    You have laid Me in the dust and left Me for
      dead.

¹⁶ My enemies surround Me like a pack of
      dogs;
    an evil gang closes in on Me.
  They have pierced My hands and feet.
¹⁷ I can count every bone in My body.
    My enemies stare at Me and gloat.
¹⁸ They divide My clothes among themselves
    and throw dice for My garments.

¹⁹ O Lord, do not stay away!
    You are My strength; come quickly to My aid!
²⁰ Rescue Me from a violent death;
    spare My precious life from these dogs.
²¹ Snatch Me from the lions' jaws,
    and from the horns of these wild oxen.

²² Then I will declare the wonder of Your name to my
      brothers and sisters.
    I will praise You among all Your people.

²³ Praise the LORD, all you who fear Him!
>> Honor Him, all you descendants of Jacob!
>> Show Him reverence, all you descendants of
>>> Israel!
²⁴ For He has not ignored the suffering of the needy.
>> He has not turned and walked away.
>> He has listened to their cries for help.

²⁵ I will praise You among all the people;
>> I will fulfill my vows in the presence of those who
>>> worship You.
²⁶ The poor will eat and be satisfied.
>> All who seek the LORD will praise Him.
>> Their hearts will rejoice with everlasting joy.
²⁷ The whole earth will acknowledge the LORD and return
>>> to Him.
>> People from every nation will bow down before
>>> Him.
²⁸ For the LORD is king!
>> He rules all the nations.

²⁹ Let the rich of the earth feast and worship.
>> Let all mortals—those born to die—bow down in His
>>> presence.
³⁰ Future generations will also serve Him.
>> Our children will hear about the wonders of the Lord.
³¹ His righteous acts will be told to those yet unborn.
>> They will hear about everything He has done.

Psalm 23

A psalm of David.

¹ The LORD is my shepherd;
    I have everything I need.
² He lets me rest in green meadows;
    He leads me beside peaceful streams.
³   He renews my strength.
 He guides me along right paths,
    bringing honor to His name.

⁴ Even when I walk
    through the dark valley of death,
 I will not be afraid,
    for You are close beside me.
 Your rod and Your staff
    protect and comfort me.

⁵ You prepare a feast for me
    in the presence of my enemies.
 You welcome me as a guest,
    anointing my head with oil.
    My cup overflows with blessings.
⁶ Surely Your goodness and unfailing love
    will pursue me
    all the days of my life,
 and I will live in the house of the LORD
    forever.

Psalm 24

A psalm of David.

¹ The earth is the LORD's, and everything in it.
   The world and all its people belong to Him.
² For He laid the earth's foundation on the seas
   and built it on the ocean depths.

³ Who may climb the mountain of the LORD?
   Who may stand in His holy place?
⁴ Only those whose hands and hearts are pure,
   who do not worship idols
   and never tell lies.
⁵ They will receive the LORD's blessing
   and have right standing with God their
      savior.
⁶ They alone may enter God's presence
   and worship the God of Israel.   *Interlude*

⁷ Open up, ancient gates!
   Open up, ancient doors,
   and let the King of glory enter.
⁸ Who is the King of glory?
   The LORD, strong and mighty,
   the LORD, invincible in battle.
⁹ Open up, ancient gates!
   Open up, ancient doors,
   and let the King of glory enter.

¹⁰ Who is the King of glory?
The LORD Almighty—
He is the King of glory.   *Interlude*

Psalm 25

A psalm of David.

¹ To You, O LORD, I lift up my soul.
²   I trust in You, my God!
  Do not let me be disgraced,
      or let my enemies rejoice in my defeat.
³ No one who trusts in You will ever be disgraced,
      but disgrace comes to those who try to deceive others.

⁴ Show me the path where I should walk, O LORD;
      point out the right road for me to follow.
⁵ Lead me by Your truth and teach me,
      for You are the God who saves me.
  All day long I put my hope in You.

⁶ Remember, O LORD, Your unfailing love and
          compassion,
  which You have shown from long ages past.
⁷ Forgive the rebellious sins of my youth;
      look instead through the eyes of Your unfailing love,
      for You are merciful, O LORD.

⁸ The LORD is good and does what is right;
   He shows the proper path to those who go astray.
⁹ He leads the humble in what is right,
   teaching them His way.
¹⁰ The LORD leads with unfailing love and faithfulness
   all those who keep His covenant and obey His decrees.

¹¹ For the honor of Your name, O LORD,
   forgive my many, many sins.
¹² Who are those who fear the LORD?
   He will show them the path they should choose.
¹³ They will live in prosperity,
   and their children will inherit the Promised Land.
¹⁴ Friendship with the LORD is reserved for those who fear
   Him.
   With them He shares the secrets of His covenant.
¹⁵ My eyes are always looking to the LORD for help,
   for He alone can rescue me from the traps of my
   enemies.

¹⁶ Turn to me and have mercy on me,
   for I am alone and in deep distress.
¹⁷ My problems go from bad to worse.
   Oh, save me from them all!
¹⁸ Feel my pain and see my trouble.
   Forgive all my sins.
¹⁹ See how many enemies I have,
   and how viciously they hate me!

²⁰ Protect me! Rescue my life from them!
   Do not let me be disgraced, for I trust in You.
²¹ May integrity and honesty protect me,
   for I put my hope in You.

²² O God, ransom Israel
   from all its troubles.

Proverbs 5

My son, pay attention to my wisdom; listen carefully to my wise counsel. ²Then you will learn to be discreet and will store up knowledge.

³The lips of an immoral woman are as sweet as honey, and her mouth is smoother than oil. ⁴But the result is as bitter as poison, sharp as a double-edged sword. ⁵Her feet go down to death; her steps lead straight to the grave. ⁶For she does not care about the path to life. She staggers down a crooked trail and doesn't even realize where it leads.

⁷So now, my sons, listen to me. Never stray from what I am about to say: ⁸Run from her! Don't go near the door of her house! ⁹If you do, you will lose your honor and hand over to merciless people everything you have achieved in life. ¹⁰Strangers will obtain your wealth, and someone else will enjoy the fruit of your labor. ¹¹Afterward you will groan in anguish when disease consumes your body, ¹²and

you will say, "How I hated discipline! If only I had not demanded my own way! [13]Oh, why didn't I listen to my teachers? Why didn't I pay attention to those who gave me instruction? [14]I have come to the brink of utter ruin, and now I must face public disgrace."

[15]Drink water from your own well—share your love only with your wife. [16]Why spill the water of your springs in public, having sex with just anyone? [17]You should reserve it for yourselves. Don't share it with strangers.

[18]Let your wife be a fountain of blessing for you. Rejoice in the wife of your youth. [19]She is a loving doe, a graceful deer. Let her breasts satisfy you always. May you always be captivated by her love. [20]Why be captivated, my son, with an immoral woman, or embrace the breasts of an adulterous woman?

[21]For the LORD sees clearly what a man does, examining every path he takes. [22]An evil man is held captive by his own sins; they are ropes that catch and hold him. [23]He will die for lack of self-control; he will be lost because of his incredible folly.

_____

_____

_____

_____

_____

_____

_____

_____

_____

_____

_____

_____

_____

_____

_____

_____

_____

_____

Notes

Psalm 26

A psalm of David.

¹ Declare me innocent, O LORD,
    for I have acted with integrity;
    I have trusted in the LORD without wavering.
² Put me on trial, LORD, and cross-examine me.
    Test my motives and affections.
³ For I am constantly aware of Your unfailing
        love,
    and I have lived according to Your truth.

⁴ I do not spend time with liars
    or go along with hypocrites.
⁵ I hate the gatherings of those who do evil,
    and I refuse to join in with the wicked.

⁶ I wash my hands to declare my innocence.
    I come to Your altar, O LORD,
⁷ singing a song of thanksgiving
    and telling of all Your miracles.
⁸ I love Your sanctuary, LORD,
    the place where Your glory shines.

⁹ Don't let me suffer the fate of sinners.
  Don't condemn me along with murderers.
¹⁰ Their hands are dirty with wicked schemes,
   and they constantly take bribes.

¹¹ But I am not like that; I do what is right.
   So in Your mercy, save me.
¹² I have taken a stand,
   and I will publicly praise the LORD.

Psalm 27

A psalm of David.

¹ The LORD is my light and my salvation—
  so why should I be afraid?
  The LORD protects me from danger—
  so why should I tremble?

² When evil people come to destroy me,
  when my enemies and foes attack me,
  they will stumble and fall.
³ Though a mighty army surrounds me,
  my heart will know no fear.
  Even if they attack me,
  I remain confident.

⁴ The one thing I ask of the LORD—
  the thing I seek most—

is to live in the house of the LORD all the days of my life,
  delighting in the LORD's perfections
  and meditating in His Temple.
5 For He will conceal me there when troubles come;
  He will hide me in His sanctuary.
  He will place me out of reach on a high rock.
6 Then I will hold my head high,
  above my enemies who surround me.
At His Tabernacle I will offer sacrifices with shouts of
    joy,
  singing and praising the LORD with music.

7 Listen to my pleading, O LORD.
  Be merciful and answer me!
8 My heart has heard You say, "Come and talk with
    Me."
  And my heart responds, "LORD, I am coming."
9 Do not hide Yourself from me.
  Do not reject Your servant in anger.
  You have always been my helper.
Don't leave me now; don't abandon me,
  O God of my salvation!
10 Even if my father and mother abandon me,
  the LORD will hold me close.

11 Teach me how to live, O LORD.
  Lead me along the path of honesty,
  for my enemies are waiting for me to fall.

¹² Do not let me fall into their hands.
>   For they accuse me of things I've never done
>   and breathe out violence against me.
¹³ Yet I am confident that I will see the LORD's
>   goodness
>   while I am here in the land of the living.

¹⁴ Wait patiently for the LORD.
>   Be brave and courageous.
>   Yes, wait patiently for the LORD.

Psalm 28

A psalm of David.

¹ O LORD, You are my rock of safety.
>   Please help me; don't refuse to answer me.
>   For if You are silent,
>   I might as well give up and die.
² Listen to my prayer for mercy
>   as I cry out to You for help,
>   as I lift my hands toward Your holy sanctuary.

³ Don't drag me away with the wicked—
>   with those who do evil—
>   those who speak friendly words to their neighbors
>   while planning evil in their hearts.

⁴ Give them the punishment they so richly
 deserve!
 Measure it out in proportion to their
 wickedness.
 Pay them back for all their evil deeds!
 Give them a taste of what they have done
 to others.
⁵ They care nothing for what the LORD has
 done
 or for what His hands have made.
 So He will tear them down like old buildings,
 and they will never be rebuilt!

⁶ Praise the LORD!
 For He has heard my cry for mercy.
⁷ The LORD is my strength, my shield from every
 danger.
 I trust in Him with all my heart.
 He helps me, and my heart is filled with
 joy.
 I burst out in songs of thanksgiving.

⁸ The LORD protects His people
 and gives victory to His anointed king.
⁹ Save Your people!
 Bless Israel, Your special possession!
 Lead them like a shepherd,
 and carry them forever in Your arms.

Psalm 29

A psalm of David.

¹ Give honor to the LORD, you angels;
  give honor to the LORD for His glory and strength.
² Give honor to the LORD for the glory of His name.
  Worship the LORD in the splendor of His holiness.

³ The voice of the LORD echoes above the sea.
  The God of glory thunders.
  The LORD thunders over the mighty sea.
⁴ The voice of the LORD is powerful;
  the voice of the LORD is full of majesty.
⁵ The voice of the LORD splits the mighty cedars;
  the LORD shatters the cedars of Lebanon.
⁶ He makes Lebanon's mountains skip like a calf
  and Mount Hermon to leap like a young bull.
⁷ The voice of the LORD strikes with lightning bolts.
⁸ The voice of the LORD makes the desert quake;
  the LORD shakes the desert of Kadesh.
⁹ The voice of the LORD twists mighty oaks
  and strips the forests bare.
 In His Temple everyone shouts, "Glory!"

¹⁰ The LORD rules over the floodwaters.
   The LORD reigns as king forever.
¹¹ The LORD gives His people strength.
   The LORD blesses them with peace.

Psalm 30

A psalm of David, sung at the dedication of the Temple.

¹ I will praise You, LORD, for You have rescued me.
  You refused to let my enemies triumph over me.
² O LORD my God, I cried out to You for help,
  and You restored my health.
³ You brought me up from the grave, O LORD.
  You kept me from falling into the pit of death.

⁴ Sing to the LORD, all you godly ones!
  Praise His holy name.
⁵ His anger lasts for a moment,
  but His favor lasts a lifetime!
Weeping may go on all night,
  but joy comes with the morning.

⁶ When I was prosperous I said,
  "Nothing can stop me now!"
⁷ Your favor, O LORD, made me as secure as a mountain.
  Then You turned away from me, and I was shattered.

⁸ I cried out to You, O LORD.
  I begged the Lord for mercy, saying,
⁹ "What will You gain if I die,
  if I sink down into the grave?
Can my dust praise You from the grave?
  Can it tell the world of Your faithfulness?

¹⁰ Hear me, LORD, and have mercy on me.
   Help me, O LORD."

¹¹ You have turned my mourning into joyful dancing.
   You have taken away my clothes of mourning and
      clothed me with joy,
¹² that I might sing praises to You and not be silent.
   O LORD my God, I will give You thanks
      forever!

Proverbs 6

My child, if you co-sign a loan for a friend or guarantee the
debt of someone you hardly know—²if you have trapped
yourself by your agreement and are caught by what you
said—³quick, get out of it if you possibly can! You have
placed yourself at your friend's mercy. Now swallow your
pride; go and beg to have your name erased. ⁴Don't put it
off. Do it now! Don't rest until you do. ⁵Save yourself like a
deer escaping from a hunter, like a bird fleeing from a net.

⁶Take a lesson from the ants, you lazybones. Learn from
their ways and be wise! ⁷Even though they have no prince,
governor, or ruler to make them work, ⁸they labor hard all
summer, gathering food for the winter. ⁹But you, lazybones, how long will you sleep? When will you wake up?

I want you to learn this lesson: ¹⁰A little extra sleep, a little more slumber, a little folding of the hands to rest—¹¹and poverty will pounce on you like a bandit; scarcity will attack you like an armed robber.

¹²Here is a description of worthless and wicked people: They are constant liars, ¹³signaling their true intentions to their friends by making signs with their eyes and feet and fingers. ¹⁴Their perverted hearts plot evil. They stir up trouble constantly. ¹⁵But they will be destroyed suddenly, broken beyond all hope of healing.

¹⁶There are six things the LORD hates—no, seven things He detests:
¹⁷ haughty eyes,
    a lying tongue,
    hands that kill the innocent,
¹⁸ a heart that plots evil,
    feet that race to do wrong,
¹⁹ a false witness who pours out lies,
    a person who sows discord among brothers.

²⁰My son, obey your father's commands, and don't neglect your mother's teaching. ²¹Keep their words always in your heart. Tie them around your neck. ²²Wherever you walk, their counsel can lead you. When you sleep, they will protect you. When you wake up in the morning, they will advise you. ²³For these commands and this teaching are a

lamp to light the way ahead of you. The correction of discipline is the way to life.

²⁴These commands and this teaching will keep you from the immoral woman, from the smooth tongue of an adulterous woman. ²⁵Don't lust for her beauty. Don't let her coyness seduce you. ²⁶For a prostitute will bring you to poverty, and sleeping with another man's wife may cost you your very life. ²⁷Can a man scoop fire into his lap and not be burned? ²⁸Can he walk on hot coals and not blister his feet? ²⁹So it is with the man who sleeps with another man's wife. He who embraces her will not go unpunished.

³⁰Excuses might be found for a thief who steals because he is starving. ³¹But if he is caught, he will be fined seven times as much as he stole, even if it means selling everything in his house to pay it back.

³²But the man who commits adultery is an utter fool, for he destroys his own soul. ³³Wounds and constant disgrace are his lot. His shame will never be erased. ³⁴For the woman's husband will be furious in his jealousy, and he will have no mercy in his day of vengeance. ³⁵There is no compensation or bribe that will satisfy him.

_____

_____

_____

_____

_____

_____

_____

_____

_____

_____

_____

_____

_____

_____

_____

_____

_____

_____

_____

_____

Psalm 31

For the choir director: A psalm of David.

¹ O LORD, I have come to You for protection;
    don't let me be put to shame.
    Rescue me, for You always do what is right.
² Bend down and listen to me;
    rescue me quickly.
  Be for me a great rock of safety,
    a fortress where my enemies cannot reach me.

³ You are my rock and my fortress.
    For the honor of Your name, lead me out of this peril.
⁴ Pull me from the trap my enemies set for me,
    for I find protection in You alone.
⁵ I entrust my spirit into Your hand.
    Rescue me, LORD, for You are a faithful God.

⁶ I hate those who worship worthless idols.
    I trust in the LORD.
⁷ I am overcome with joy because of Your unfailing love,
    for You have seen my troubles,
    and You care about the anguish of my soul.

⁸ You have not handed me over to my enemy
    but have set me in a safe place.

⁹ Have mercy on me, LORD, for I am in distress.
    My sight is blurred because of my tears.
    My body and soul are withering away.
¹⁰ I am dying from grief;
    my years are shortened by sadness.
  Misery has drained my strength;
    I am wasting away from within.
¹¹ I am scorned by all my enemies
    and despised by my neighbors—
  even my friends are afraid to come near me.
  When they see me on the street,
    they turn the other way.
¹² I have been ignored as if I were dead,
    as if I were a broken pot.
¹³ I have heard the many rumors about me,
    and I am surrounded by terror.
  My enemies conspire against me,
    plotting to take my life.

¹⁴ But I am trusting You, O LORD,
    saying, "You are my God!"
¹⁵ My future is in Your hands.
    Rescue me from those who hunt me down relentlessly.
¹⁶ Let Your favor shine on Your servant.
    In Your unfailing love, save me.

¹⁷ Don't let me be disgraced, O LORD,
    for I call out to You for help.
  Let the wicked be disgraced;
    let them lie silent in the grave.
¹⁸ May their lying lips be silenced—
    those proud and arrogant lips that accuse the godly.

¹⁹ Your goodness is so great!
    You have stored up great blessings for those who honor
      You.
  You have done so much for those who come to You for
      protection,
    blessing them before the watching world.
²⁰ You hide them in the shelter of Your presence,
    safe from those who conspire against them.
  You shelter them in Your presence,
    far from accusing tongues.

²¹ Praise the LORD,
    for He has shown me His unfailing love.
    He kept me safe when my city was under attack.
²² In sudden fear I had cried out,
    "I have been cut off from the LORD!"
  But You heard my cry for mercy
    and answered my call for help.

²³ Love the LORD, all you faithful ones!
    For the LORD protects those who are loyal to Him,

but He harshly punishes all who are arrogant.
²⁴ So be strong and take courage,
    all you who put your hope in the LORD!

Psalm 32

A psalm of David.

¹ Oh, what joy for those
    whose rebellion is forgiven,
    whose sin is put out of sight!
² Yes, what joy for those
    whose record the LORD has cleared of sin,
    whose lives are lived in complete honesty!

³ When I refused to confess my sin,
    I was weak and miserable,
    and I groaned all day long.
⁴ Day and night Your hand of discipline was heavy on me.
    My strength evaporated like water in the summer heat.

Interlude

⁵ Finally, I confessed all my sins to You
    and stopped trying to hide them.
  I said to myself, "I will confess my rebellion to the
      LORD."
    And You forgave me! All my guilt is gone.

Interlude

⁶ Therefore, let all the godly confess their rebellion to You
     while there is time,
   that they may not drown in the floodwaters of
     judgment.
⁷ For You are my hiding place;
   You protect me from trouble.
   You surround me with songs of victory.

Interlude

⁸ The LORD says, "I will guide you along the best pathway
     for your life.
   I will advise you and watch over you.
⁹ Do not be like a senseless horse or mule
   that needs a bit and bridle to keep it under control."

¹⁰ Many sorrows come to the wicked,
     but unfailing love surrounds those who trust the
     LORD.
¹¹ So rejoice in the LORD and be glad, all you who obey
     Him!
   Shout for joy, all you whose hearts are pure!

Psalm 33

¹ Let the godly sing with joy to the LORD,
   for it is fitting to praise Him.

²Praise the LORD with melodies on the lyre;
   make music for Him on the ten-stringed harp.
³Sing new songs of praise to Him;
   play skillfully on the harp and sing with joy.

⁴For the word of the LORD holds true,
   and everything He does is worthy of our trust.
⁵He loves whatever is just and good,
   and His unfailing love fills the earth.

⁶The LORD merely spoke,
   and the heavens were created.
 He breathed the word,
   and all the stars were born.
⁷He gave the sea its boundaries
   and locked the oceans in vast reservoirs.

⁸Let everyone in the world fear the LORD,
   and let everyone stand in awe of Him.
⁹For when He spoke, the world began!
   It appeared at His command.

¹⁰The LORD shatters the plans of the nations
   and thwarts all their schemes.
¹¹But the LORD's plans stand firm forever;
   His intentions can never be shaken.

¹²What joy for the nation whose God is the LORD,
   whose people He has chosen for His own.

¹³ The LORD looks down from heaven
>   and sees the whole human race.
¹⁴ From His throne He observes
>   all who live on the earth.
¹⁵ He made their hearts,
>   so He understands everything they do.
¹⁶ The best-equipped army cannot save
>   a king,
>   nor is great strength enough to save a
>   warrior.
¹⁷ Don't count on your warhorse to give you
>   victory—
>   for all its strength, it cannot save you.

¹⁸ But the LORD watches over those who fear
>   Him,
>   those who rely on His unfailing love.
¹⁹ He rescues them from death
>   and keeps them alive in times of famine.

²⁰ We depend on the LORD alone to save us.
>   Only He can help us, protecting us like a
>   shield.
²¹ In Him our hearts rejoice,
>   for we are trusting in His holy name.
²² Let Your unfailing love surround us,
>   LORD,
>   for our hope is in You alone.

Psalm 34

A psalm of David, regarding the time he pretended to be insane in front of Abimelech, who sent him away.

¹ I will praise the LORD at all times.
    I will constantly speak His praises.
² I will boast only in the LORD;
    let all who are discouraged take heart.
³ Come, let us tell of the LORD's greatness;
    let us exalt His name together.

⁴ I prayed to the LORD, and He answered me,
    freeing me from all my fears.
⁵ Those who look to Him for help will be radiant with joy;
    no shadow of shame will darken their faces.
⁶ I cried out to the LORD in my suffering, and He heard
    me.
    He set me free from all my fears.
⁷ For the angel of the LORD guards all who fear Him,
    and He rescues them.

⁸ Taste and see that the LORD is good.
    Oh, the joys of those who trust in Him!
⁹ Let the LORD's people show Him reverence,
    for those who honor Him will have all they need.
¹⁰ Even strong young lions sometimes go hungry,
    but those who trust in the LORD will never lack any
    good thing.

¹¹ Come, my children, and listen to me,
    and I will teach you to fear the LORD.
¹² Do any of you want to live
    a life that is long and good?
¹³ Then watch your tongue!
    Keep your lips from telling lies!
¹⁴ Turn away from evil and do good.
    Work hard at living in peace with others.

¹⁵ The eyes of the LORD watch over those who do right;
    His ears are open to their cries for help.
¹⁶ But the LORD turns His face against those who do evil;
    He will erase their memory from the earth.

¹⁷ The LORD hears His people when they call to Him for
    help.
    He rescues them from all their troubles.
¹⁸ The LORD is close to the brokenhearted;
    He rescues those who are crushed in spirit.

¹⁹ The righteous face many troubles,
    but the LORD rescues them from each and every one.
²⁰ For the LORD protects them from harm—
    not one of their bones will be broken!

²¹ Calamity will surely overtake the wicked,
    and those who hate the righteous will be punished.
²² But the LORD will redeem those who serve Him.
    Everyone who trusts in Him will be freely pardoned.

Psalm 35

A psalm of David.

¹ O LORD, oppose those who oppose me.
  Declare war on those who are attacking me.
² Put on Your armor, and take up Your shield.
  Prepare for battle, and come to my aid.
³ Lift up Your spear and javelin
  and block the way of my enemies.
 Let me hear You say,
  "I am your salvation!"

⁴ Humiliate and disgrace those trying to kill me;
  turn them back in confusion.
⁵ Blow them away like chaff in the wind—
  a wind sent by the angel of the LORD.
⁶ Make their path dark and slippery,
  with the angel of the LORD pursuing them.
⁷ Although I did them no wrong,
  they laid a trap for me.
 Although I did them no wrong,
  they dug a pit for me.
⁸ So let sudden ruin overtake them!
  Let them be caught in the snare they set for me!
  Let them fall to destruction in the pit they dug for me.

⁹ Then I will rejoice in the LORD.
  I will be glad because He rescues me.

¹⁰ I will praise Him from the bottom of my heart:
　　"LORD, who can compare with You?
　Who else rescues the weak and helpless from the
　　　　strong?
　　Who else protects the poor and needy from those who
　　　want to rob them?"

¹¹ Malicious witnesses testify against me.
　　They accuse me of things I don't even know about.
¹² They repay me with evil for the good I do.
　　I am sick with despair.
¹³ Yet when they were ill,
　　I grieved for them.
　I even fasted and prayed for them,
　　but my prayers returned unanswered.
¹⁴ I was sad, as though they were my friends or family,
　　as if I were grieving for my own mother.

¹⁵ But they are glad now that I am in trouble;
　　they gleefully join together against me.
　I am attacked by people I don't even know;
　　they hurl slander at me continually.
¹⁶ They mock me with the worst kind of profanity,
　　and they snarl at me.

¹⁷ How long, O Lord, will You look on and do nothing?
　　Rescue me from their fierce attacks.
　　Protect my life from these lions!

¹⁸ Then I will thank You in front of the entire
     congregation.
  I will praise You before all the people.

¹⁹ Don't let my treacherous enemies
    rejoice over my defeat.
 Don't let those who hate me without cause
    gloat over my sorrow.
²⁰ They don't talk of peace;
    they plot against innocent people
    who are minding their own business.
²¹ They shout that they have seen me doing wrong.
    "Aha," they say. "Aha!
    With our own eyes we saw him do it!"

²² O Lord, You know all about this.
    Do not stay silent.
    Don't abandon me now, O Lord.
²³ Wake up! Rise to my defense!
    Take up my case, my God and my Lord.
²⁴ Declare me "not guilty," O Lord my God, for You give
     justice.
    Don't let my enemies laugh about me in my troubles.
²⁵ Don't let them say, "Look! We have what we wanted!
    Now we will eat him alive!"

²⁶ May those who rejoice at my troubles
    be humiliated and disgraced.

May those who triumph over me
    be covered with shame and dishonor.

27 But give great joy to those
    who have stood with me in my defense.
Let them continually say, "Great is the LORD,
    who enjoys helping His servant."
28 Then I will tell everyone of Your justice and goodness,
    and I will praise You all day long.

Proverbs 7

Follow my advice, my son; always treasure my commands.
²Obey them and live! Guard my teachings as your most
precious possession. ³Tie them on your fingers as a
reminder. Write them deep within your heart.

⁴Love wisdom like a sister; make insight a beloved
member of your family. ⁵Let them hold you back from an
affair with an immoral woman, from listening to the flattery of an adulterous woman.

⁶I was looking out the window of my house one day ⁷and
saw a simpleminded young man who lacked common
sense. ⁸He was crossing the street near the house of an
immoral woman. He was strolling down the path by her
house ⁹at twilight, as the day was fading, as the dark of
night set in. ¹⁰The woman approached him, dressed seduc-

tively and sly of heart. ¹¹She was the brash, rebellious type who never stays at home. ¹²She is often seen in the streets and markets, soliciting at every corner.

¹³She threw her arms around him and kissed him, and with a brazen look she said, ¹⁴"I've offered my sacrifices and just finished my vows. ¹⁵It's you I was looking for! I came out to find you, and here you are! ¹⁶My bed is spread with colored sheets of finest linen imported from Egypt. ¹⁷I've perfumed my bed with myrrh, aloes, and cinnamon. ¹⁸Come, let's drink our fill of love until morning. Let's enjoy each other's caresses, ¹⁹for my husband is not home. He's away on a long trip. ²⁰He has taken a wallet full of money with him, and he won't return until later in the month."

²¹So she seduced him with her pretty speech. With her flattery she enticed him. ²²He followed her at once, like an ox going to the slaughter or like a trapped stag, ²³awaiting the arrow that would pierce its heart. He was like a bird flying into a snare, little knowing it would cost him his life.

²⁴Listen to me, my sons, and pay attention to my words. ²⁵Don't let your hearts stray away toward her. Don't wander down her wayward path. ²⁶For she has been the ruin of many; numerous men have been her victims. ²⁷Her house is the road to the grave. Her bedroom is the den of death.

Notes

Psalm 36

For the choir director: A psalm of David, the servant of the LORD.

¹ Sin whispers to the wicked, deep within their hearts.
   They have no fear of God to restrain them.
² In their blind conceit,
   they cannot see how wicked they really are.
³ Everything they say is crooked and deceitful.
   They refuse to act wisely or do what is good.
⁴ They lie awake at night, hatching sinful plots.
   Their course of action is never good.
   They make no attempt to turn from evil.

⁵ Your unfailing love, O LORD, is as vast as the heavens;
   Your faithfulness reaches beyond the clouds.
⁶ Your righteousness is like the mighty mountains,
   Your justice like the ocean depths.
   You care for people and animals alike, O LORD.
⁷   How precious is Your unfailing love, O God!
   All humanity finds shelter
      in the shadow of Your wings.
⁸ You feed them from the abundance of Your own house,
   letting them drink from Your rivers of delight.

⁹ For You are the fountain of life,
    the light by which we see.

¹⁰ Pour out Your unfailing love on those who love You;
    give justice to those with honest hearts.
¹¹ Don't let the proud trample me;
    don't let the wicked push me around.
¹² Look! They have fallen!
    They have been thrown down, never to rise again.

Psalm 37

A psalm of David.

¹ Don't worry about the wicked.
    Don't envy those who do wrong.
² For like grass, they soon fade away.
    Like springtime flowers, they soon wither.

³ Trust in the LORD and do good.
    Then you will live safely in the land and prosper.
⁴ Take delight in the LORD,
    and He will give you your heart's desires.

⁵ Commit everything you do to the LORD.
    Trust Him, and He will help you.
⁶ He will make your innocence as clear as the dawn,
    and the justice of your cause will shine like the
        noonday sun.

⁷ Be still in the presence of the LORD,
   and wait patiently for Him to act.
 Don't worry about evil people who prosper
   or fret about their wicked schemes.

⁸ Stop your anger!
   Turn from your rage!
 Do not envy others—
   it only leads to harm.
⁹ For the wicked will be destroyed,
   but those who trust in the LORD will possess the land.

¹⁰ In a little while, the wicked will disappear.
   Though you look for them, they will be gone.
¹¹ Those who are gentle and lowly will possess the land;
   they will live in prosperous security.

¹² The wicked plot against the godly;
   they snarl at them in defiance.
¹³ But the Lord just laughs,
   for He sees their day of judgment coming.

¹⁴ The wicked draw their swords
   and string their bows
 to kill the poor and the oppressed,
   to slaughter those who do right.
¹⁵ But they will be stabbed through the heart with their
      own swords,
   and their bows will be broken.

¹⁶ It is better to be godly and have little
     than to be evil and possess much.
¹⁷ For the strength of the wicked will be shattered,
     but the LORD takes care of the godly.

¹⁸ Day by day the LORD takes care of the innocent,
     and they will receive a reward that lasts forever.
¹⁹ They will survive through hard times;
     even in famine they will have more than enough.

²⁰ But the wicked will perish.
     The LORD's enemies are like flowers in a field—
     they will disappear like smoke.

²¹ The wicked borrow and never repay,
     but the godly are generous givers.
²² Those blessed by the LORD will inherit the land,
     but those cursed by Him will die.

²³ The steps of the godly are directed by the LORD.
     He delights in every detail of their lives.
²⁴ Though they stumble, they will not fall,
     for the LORD holds them by the hand.

²⁵ Once I was young, and now I am old.
     Yet I have never seen the godly forsaken,
     nor seen their children begging for bread.
²⁶ The godly always give generous loans to others,
     and their children are a blessing.

²⁷ Turn from evil and do good,
   and you will live in the land forever.
²⁸ For the LORD loves justice,
   and He will never abandon the godly.

He will keep them safe forever,
   but the children of the wicked will perish.
²⁹ The godly will inherit the land
   and will live there forever.

³⁰ The godly offer good counsel;
   they know what is right from wrong.
³¹ They fill their hearts with God's law,
   so they will never slip from His path.

³² Those who are evil spy on the godly,
   waiting for an excuse to kill them.
³³ But the LORD will not let the wicked succeed
   or let the godly be condemned when they are brought
      before the judge.

³⁴ Don't be impatient for the LORD to act!
   Travel steadily along His path.
He will honor you, giving you the land.
   You will see the wicked destroyed.

³⁵ I myself have seen it happen—
   proud and evil people thriving like mighty trees.
³⁶ But when I looked again, they were gone!
   Though I searched for them, I could not find them!

³⁷ Look at those who are honest and good,
   for a wonderful future lies before those who love peace.
³⁸ But the wicked will be destroyed;
   they have no future.

³⁹ The LORD saves the godly;
   He is their fortress in times of trouble.
⁴⁰ The LORD helps them,
   rescuing them from the wicked.
 He saves them,
   and they find shelter in Him.

Psalm 38

A psalm of David, to bring us to the LORD's remembrance.

¹ O LORD, don't rebuke me in Your anger!
   Don't discipline me in Your rage!
² Your arrows have struck deep,
   and Your blows are crushing me.

³ Because of Your anger, my whole body is sick;
   my health is broken because of my sins.
⁴ My guilt overwhelms me—
   it is a burden too heavy to bear.
⁵ My wounds fester and stink
   because of my foolish sins.

⁶ I am bent over and racked with pain.
   My days are filled with grief.
⁷ A raging fever burns within me,
   and my health is broken.
⁸ I am exhausted and completely crushed.
   My groans come from an anguished heart.

⁹ You know what I long for, Lord;
   You hear my every sigh.
¹⁰ My heart beats wildly, my strength fails,
   and I am going blind.
¹¹ My loved ones and friends stay away, fearing my disease.
   Even my own family stands at a distance.
¹² Meanwhile, my enemies lay traps for me;
   they make plans to ruin me.
   They think up treacherous deeds all day long.
¹³ But I am deaf to all their threats.
   I am silent before them as one who cannot speak.
¹⁴ I choose to hear nothing,
   and I make no reply.

¹⁵ For I am waiting for You, O LORD.
   You must answer for me, O Lord my God.
¹⁶ I prayed, "Don't let my enemies gloat over me
   or rejoice at my downfall."
¹⁷ I am on the verge of collapse,
   facing constant pain.
¹⁸ But I confess my sins;

I am deeply sorry for what I have done.
¹⁹ My enemies are many;
    they hate me though I have done nothing against them.
²⁰ They repay me evil for good
    and oppose me because I stand for the right.

²¹ Do not abandon me, LORD.
    Do not stand at a distance, my God.
²² Come quickly to help me, O Lord my savior.

Psalm 39

For Jeduthun, the choir director: A psalm of David.

¹ I said to myself, "I will watch what I do
    and not sin in what I say.
 I will curb my tongue
    when the ungodly are around me."
² But as I stood there in silence—
    not even speaking of good things—
    the turmoil within me grew to the bursting point.
³ My thoughts grew hot within me
    and began to burn,
    igniting a fire of words:
⁴ "LORD, remind me how brief my time on earth will be.
    Remind me that my days are numbered,
    and that my life is fleeing away.

⁵ My life is no longer than the width of my hand.
     An entire lifetime is just a moment to You;
     human existence is but a breath."   *Interlude*

⁶ We are merely moving shadows,
     and all our busy rushing ends in nothing.
     We heap up wealth for someone else to spend.

⁷ And so, Lord, where do I put my hope?
     My only hope is in You.
⁸ Rescue me from my rebellion,
     for even fools mock me when I rebel.
⁹ I am silent before You; I won't say a word.
     For my punishment is from You.
¹⁰ Please, don't punish me anymore!
     I am exhausted by the blows from Your hand.
¹¹ When You discipline people for their sins,
     their lives can be crushed like the life of a moth.
     Human existence is as frail as breath.   *Interlude*

¹² Hear my prayer, O LORD!
     Listen to my cries for help!
     Don't ignore my tears.
   For I am Your guest—
     a traveler passing through,
     as my ancestors were before me.
¹³ Spare me so I can smile again
     before I am gone and exist no more.

Psalm 40

For the choir director: A psalm of David.

¹ I waited patiently for the LORD to help me,
  and He turned to me and heard my cry.
² He lifted me out of the pit of despair,
  out of the mud and the mire.
 He set my feet on solid ground
  and steadied me as I walked along.
³ He has given me a new song to sing,
  a hymn of praise to our God.
 Many will see what He has done and be astounded.
  They will put their trust in the LORD.

⁴ Oh, the joys of those who trust the LORD,
  who have no confidence in the proud,
  or in those who worship idols.
⁵ O LORD my God, You have done many miracles for us.
  Your plans for us are too numerous to list.
 If I tried to recite all Your wonderful deeds,
  I would never come to the end of them.

⁶ You take no delight in sacrifices or offerings.
  Now that You have made me listen, I finally
   understand—
  You don't require burnt offerings or sin offerings.
⁷ Then I said, "Look, I have come.
  And this has been written about me in Your scroll:

⁸ I take joy in doing Your will, my God,
    for Your law is written on my heart."

⁹ I have told all Your people about Your justice.
    I have not been afraid to speak out,
    as You, O LORD, well know.
¹⁰ I have not kept this good news hidden in my heart;
    I have talked about Your faithfulness and saving
        power.
  I have told everyone in the great assembly
    of Your unfailing love and faithfulness.

¹¹ LORD, don't hold back Your tender mercies from me.
    My only hope is in Your unfailing love and
        faithfulness.
¹² For troubles surround me—
    too many to count!
  They pile up so high
    I can't see my way out.
  They are more numerous than the hairs on my head.
    I have lost all my courage.

¹³ Please, LORD, rescue me!
    Come quickly, LORD, and help me.
¹⁴ May those who try to destroy me
    be humiliated and put to shame.
  May those who take delight in my trouble
    be turned back in disgrace.

¹⁵ Let them be horrified by their shame,
    for they said, "Aha! We've got him now!"

¹⁶ But may all who search for You
    be filled with joy and gladness.
  May those who love Your salvation
    repeatedly shout, "The LORD is great!"

¹⁷ As for me, I am poor and needy,
    but the Lord is thinking about me right now.
  You are my helper and my savior.
    Do not delay, O my God.

Proverbs 8

Listen as wisdom calls out! Hear as understanding raises
her voice! ²She stands on the hilltop and at the crossroads.
³At the entrance to the city, at the city gates, she cries aloud,
⁴"I call to you, to all of you! I am raising my voice to all
people. ⁵How naive you are! Let me give you common
sense. O foolish ones, let me give you understanding.
⁶Listen to me! For I have excellent things to tell you.
Everything I say is right, ⁷for I speak the truth and hate
every kind of deception. ⁸My advice is wholesome and
good. There is nothing crooked or twisted in it. ⁹My words
are plain to anyone with understanding, clear to those who
want to learn.

¹⁰"Choose my instruction rather than silver, and knowledge over pure gold. ¹¹For wisdom is far more valuable than rubies. Nothing you desire can be compared with it.

¹²"I, Wisdom, live together with good judgment. I know where to discover knowledge and discernment. ¹³All who fear the LORD will hate evil. That is why I hate pride, arrogance, corruption, and perverted speech. ¹⁴Good advice and success belong to me. Insight and strength are mine. ¹⁵Because of me, kings reign, and rulers make just laws. ¹⁶Rulers lead with my help, and nobles make righteous judgments.

¹⁷"I love all who love me. Those who search for me will surely find me. ¹⁸Unending riches, honor, wealth, and justice are mine to distribute. ¹⁹My gifts are better than the purest gold, my wages better than sterling silver! ²⁰I walk in righteousness, in paths of justice. ²¹Those who love me inherit wealth, for I fill their treasuries.

²²"The LORD formed me from the beginning, before He created anything else. ²³I was appointed in ages past, at the very first, before the earth began. ²⁴I was born before the oceans were created, before the springs bubbled forth their waters. ²⁵Before the mountains and the hills were formed, I was born—²⁶before He had made the earth and fields and the first handfuls of soil.

²⁷"I was there when He established the heavens, when He drew the horizon on the oceans. ²⁸I was there when He set the clouds above, when He established the deep foun-

tains of the earth. ²⁹I was there when He set the limits of the seas, so they would not spread beyond their boundaries. And when He marked off the earth's foundations, ³⁰I was the architect at His side. I was His constant delight, rejoicing always in His presence. ³¹And how happy I was with what He created—His wide world and all the human family!

³²"And so, my children, listen to me, for happy are all who follow my ways. ³³Listen to my counsel and be wise. Don't ignore it.

³⁴"Happy are those who listen to me, watching for me daily at my gates, waiting for me outside my home! ³⁵For whoever finds me finds life and wins approval from the LORD. ³⁶But those who miss me have injured themselves. All who hate me love death."

Notes

Notes

Psalm 41

For the choir director: A psalm of David.

¹ Oh, the joys of those who are kind to the poor.
    The LORD rescues them in times of trouble.
² The LORD protects them
    and keeps them alive.
 He gives them prosperity
    and rescues them from their enemies.
³ The LORD nurses them when they are sick
    and eases their pain and discomfort.

⁴ "O LORD," I prayed, "have mercy on me.
    Heal me, for I have sinned against You."
⁵ But my enemies say nothing but evil about me.
    "How soon will he die and be forgotten?" they ask.
⁶ They visit me as if they are my friends,
    but all the while they gather gossip,
    and when they leave, they spread it everywhere.
⁷ All who hate me whisper about me,
    imagining the worst for me.
⁸ "Whatever he has, it is fatal," they say.
    "He will never get out of that bed!"

⁹ Even my best friend, the one I trusted completely,
    the one who shared my food,
    has turned against me.

¹⁰ LORD, have mercy on me.
    Make me well again, so I can pay them back!
¹¹ I know that You are pleased with me,
    for You have not let my enemy triumph over me.
¹² You have preserved my life because I am innocent;
    You have brought me into Your presence forever.

¹³ Bless the LORD, the God of Israel,
    who lives forever from eternal ages past.
    Amen and amen!

Psalm 42

For the choir director: A psalm of the descendants of Korah.

¹ As the deer pants for streams of water,
    so I long for You, O God.
² I thirst for God, the living God.
    When can I come and stand before Him?
³ Day and night, I have only tears for food,
    while my enemies continually taunt me, saying,
    "Where is this God of yours?"

⁴ My heart is breaking
    as I remember how it used to be:

I walked among the crowds of worshipers,
    leading a great procession to the house of God,
singing for joy and giving thanks—
    it was the sound of a great celebration!

⁵ Why am I discouraged?
    Why so sad?
I will put my hope in God!
    I will praise Him again—
    my Savior and ⁶my God!

Now I am deeply discouraged,
    but I will remember Your kindness—
from Mount Hermon, the source of the Jordan,
    from the land of Mount Mizar.
⁷ I hear the tumult of the raging seas
    as Your waves and surging tides sweep over me.

⁸ Through each day the LORD pours His unfailing love
        upon me,
    and through each night I sing His songs,
    praying to God who gives me life.

⁹ "O God my rock," I cry,
    "Why have You forsaken me?
  Why must I wander in darkness,
    oppressed by my enemies?"
¹⁰ Their taunts pierce me like a fatal wound.
    They scoff, "Where is this God of yours?"

[11] Why am I discouraged?
    Why so sad?
  I will put my hope in God!
    I will praise Him again—
    my Savior and my God!

Psalm 43

[1] O God, take up my cause!
    Defend me against these ungodly people.
    Rescue me from these unjust liars.
[2] For You are God, my only safe haven.
    Why have You tossed me aside?
  Why must I wander around in darkness,
    oppressed by my enemies?

[3] Send out Your light and Your truth;
    let them guide me.
  Let them lead me to Your holy mountain,
    to the place where You live.
[4] There I will go to the altar of God,
    to God—the source of all my joy.
  I will praise You with my harp,
    O God, my God!

[5] Why am I discouraged?
    Why so sad?

I will put my hope in God!
   I will praise Him again—
      my Savior and my God!

Psalm 44

For the choir director: A psalm of the descendants of Korah.

¹ O God, we have heard it with our own ears—
   our ancestors have told us
of all You did in other days,
   in days long ago:
² You drove out the pagan nations
   and gave all the land to our ancestors;
You crushed their enemies,
   setting our ancestors free.
³ They did not conquer the land with their swords;
   it was not their own strength that gave them victory.
It was by Your mighty power that they succeeded;
   it was because You favored them and smiled on them.

⁴ You are my King and my God.
   You command victories for Your people.
⁵ Only by Your power can we push back our enemies;
   only in Your name can we trample our foes.
⁶ I do not trust my bow;
   I do not count on my sword to save me.

⁷ It is You who gives us victory over our enemies;
    it is You who humbles those who hate us.
⁸ O God, we give glory to You all day long
    and constantly praise Your name.   *Interlude*

⁹ But now You have tossed us aside in dishonor.
    You no longer lead our armies to battle.
¹⁰ You make us retreat from our enemies
    and allow them to plunder our land.
¹¹ You have treated us like sheep waiting to be slaughtered;
    You have scattered us among the nations.
¹² You sold us—Your precious people—for a pittance.
    You valued us at nothing at all.

¹³ You have caused all our neighbors to mock us.
    We are an object of scorn and derision to the nations
        around us.
¹⁴ You have made us the butt of their jokes;
    we are scorned by the whole world.
¹⁵ We can't escape the constant humiliation;
    shame is written across our faces.
¹⁶ All we hear are the taunts of our mockers.
    All we see are our vengeful enemies.

¹⁷ All this has happened despite our loyalty to You.
    We have not violated Your covenant.
¹⁸ Our hearts have not deserted You.
    We have not strayed from Your path.

¹⁹ Yet You have crushed us in the desert.
    You have covered us with darkness and death.

²⁰ If we had turned away from worshiping our God
    or spread our hands in prayer to foreign gods,
²¹ God would surely have known it,
    for He knows the secrets of every heart.
²² For Your sake we are killed every day;
    we are being slaughtered like sheep.

²³ Wake up, O Lord! Why do You sleep?
    Get up! Do not reject us forever.
²⁴ Why do You look the other way?
    Why do You ignore our suffering and oppression?
²⁵ We collapse in the dust,
    lying face down in the dirt.
²⁶ Rise up! Come and help us!
    Save us because of Your unfailing love.

Psalm 45

For the choir director: A psalm of the descendants of Korah, to be sung to the tune "Lilies." A love song.

¹ My heart overflows with a beautiful thought!
    I will recite a lovely poem to the king,
        for my tongue is like the pen of a skillful poet.

²You are the most handsome of all.
  Gracious words stream from Your lips.
  God Himself has blessed You forever.
³Put on Your sword, O mighty warrior!
  You are so glorious, so majestic!
⁴In Your majesty, ride out to victory,
  defending truth, humility, and justice.
  Go forth to perform awe-inspiring deeds!
⁵Your arrows are sharp,
  piercing Your enemies' hearts.
The nations fall before You,
  lying down beneath Your feet.

⁶Your throne, O God, endures forever and ever.
  Your royal power is expressed in justice.
⁷You love what is right and hate what is wrong.
  Therefore God, Your God, has anointed You,
  pouring out the oil of joy on You more than on anyone
    else.
⁸Your robes are perfumed with myrrh, aloes, and cassia.
  In palaces decorated with ivory,
  You are entertained by the music of harps.
⁹Kings' daughters are among Your concubines.
  At Your right side stands the queen,
  wearing jewelry of finest gold from Ophir!

¹⁰Listen to me, O royal daughter; take to heart what I say.
  Forget your people and your homeland far away.

¹¹ For your royal husband delights in your beauty;
   honor Him, for He is your Lord.
¹² The princes of Tyre will shower you with gifts.
   People of great wealth will entreat your favor.

¹³ The bride, a princess, waits within her chamber,
   dressed in a gown woven with gold.
¹⁴ In her beautiful robes, she is led to the King,
   accompanied by her bridesmaids.
¹⁵ What a joyful, enthusiastic procession
   as they enter the king's palace!

¹⁶ Your sons will become kings like their father.
   You will make them rulers over many lands.

¹⁷ I will bring honor to Your name in every generation.
   Therefore, the nations will praise You forever and
      ever.

Proverbs 9

Wisdom has built her spacious house with seven pillars.
²She has prepared a great banquet, mixed the wines, and
set the table. ³She has sent her servants to invite everyone to
come. She calls out from the heights overlooking the city.
⁴"Come home with me," she urges the simple. To those
without good judgment, she says, ⁵"Come, eat my food,

and drink the wine I have mixed. ⁶Leave your foolish ways behind, and begin to live; learn how to be wise."

⁷Anyone who rebukes a mocker will get a smart retort. Anyone who rebukes the wicked will get hurt. ⁸So don't bother rebuking mockers; they will only hate you. But the wise, when rebuked, will love you all the more. ⁹Teach the wise, and they will be wiser. Teach the righteous, and they will learn more.

¹⁰Fear of the LORD is the beginning of wisdom. Knowledge of the Holy One results in understanding.

¹¹Wisdom will multiply your days and add years to your life. ¹²If you become wise, you will be the one to benefit. If you scorn wisdom, you will be the one to suffer.

¹³The woman named Folly is loud and brash. She is ignorant and doesn't even know it. ¹⁴She sits in her doorway on the heights overlooking the city. ¹⁵She calls out to men going by who are minding their own business. ¹⁶"Come home with me," she urges the simple. To those without good judgment, she says, ¹⁷"Stolen water is refreshing; food eaten in secret tastes the best!" ¹⁸But the men don't realize that her former guests are now in the grave.

Notes

Notes

Psalm 46

For the choir director: A psalm of the descendants of Korah, to be sung by soprano voices. A song.

¹ God is our refuge and strength,
    always ready to help in times of trouble.
² So we will not fear, even if earthquakes come
    and the mountains crumble into the sea.
³ Let the oceans roar and foam.
    Let the mountains tremble as the waters surge!

Interlude

⁴ A river brings joy to the city of our God,
    the sacred home of the Most High.
⁵ God Himself lives in that city; it cannot be destroyed.
    God will protect it at the break of day.
⁶ The nations are in an uproar,
    and kingdoms crumble!
  God thunders,
    and the earth melts!

⁷ The LORD Almighty is here among us;
    the God of Israel is our fortress.   *Interlude*

⁸ Come, see the glorious works of the LORD:
    See how He brings destruction upon the
        world
⁹ and causes wars to end throughout the earth.
    He breaks the bow and snaps the spear in two;
    He burns the shields with fire.

¹⁰ "Be silent, and know that I am God!
    I will be honored by every nation.
    I will be honored throughout the world."

¹¹ The LORD Almighty is here among us;
    the God of Israel is our fortress.   *Interlude*

Psalm 47

For the choir director: A psalm of the descendants of Korah.

¹ Come, everyone, and clap your hands for joy!
    Shout to God with joyful praise!
² For the LORD Most High is awesome.
    He is the great King of all the earth.
³ He subdues the nations before us,
    putting our enemies beneath our feet.
⁴ He chose the Promised Land as our inheritance,
    the proud possession of Jacob's descendants, whom He
        loves.   *Interlude*

⁵ God has ascended with a mighty shout.
  The LORD has ascended with trumpets blaring.
⁶ Sing praise to God, sing praises;
  sing praise to our King, sing praises!

⁷ For God is the King over all the earth.
  Praise Him with a psalm!
⁸ God reigns above the nations,
  sitting on His holy throne.
⁹ The rulers of the world have gathered together.
  They join us in praising the God of Abraham.
For all the kings of the earth belong to God.
  He is highly honored everywhere.

Psalm 48

A psalm of the descendants of Korah. A song.

¹ How great is the LORD,
  and how much we should praise Him
in the city of our God,
  which is on His holy mountain!
² It is magnificent in elevation—
  the whole earth rejoices to see it!
Mount Zion, the holy mountain,
  is the city of the great King!

³ God Himself is in Jerusalem's towers.
    He reveals Himself as her defender.

⁴ The kings of the earth joined forces
    and advanced against the city.
⁵ But when they saw it, they were stunned;
    they were terrified and ran away.
⁶ They were gripped with terror,
    like a woman writhing in the pain of
        childbirth
⁷ or like the mighty ships of Tarshish
    being shattered by a powerful east wind.

⁸ We had heard of the city's glory,
    but now we have seen it ourselves—
    the city of the LORD Almighty.
  It is the city of our God;
    He will make it safe forever.   *Interlude*

⁹ O God, we meditate on Your unfailing love
    as we worship in Your Temple.
¹⁰ As Your name deserves, O God,
    You will be praised to the ends of the earth.
    Your strong right hand is filled with
        victory.
¹¹ Let the people on Mount Zion rejoice.
    Let the towns of Judah be glad,
    for Your judgments are just.

¹² Go, inspect the city of Jerusalem.
    Walk around and count the many towers.
¹³ Take note of the fortified walls,
    and tour all the citadels,
  that you may describe them
    to future generations.
¹⁴ For that is what God is like.
    He is our God forever and ever,
    and He will be our guide until we die.

Psalm 49

For the choir director: A psalm of the descendants of Korah.

¹ Listen to this, all you people!
    Pay attention, everyone in the world!
² High and low,
    rich and poor—listen!
³ For my words are wise,
    and my thoughts are filled with insight.
⁴ I listen carefully to many proverbs
    and solve riddles with inspiration from a harp.

⁵ There is no need to fear when times of trouble come,
    when enemies are surrounding me.
⁶ They trust in their wealth
    and boast of great riches.

⁷ Yet they cannot redeem themselves from
       death
    by paying a ransom to God.
⁸ Redemption does not come so easily,
    for no one can ever pay enough
⁹ to live forever
    and never see the grave.

¹⁰ Those who are wise must finally die,
    just like the foolish and senseless,
    leaving all their wealth behind.
¹¹ The grave is their eternal home,
    where they will stay forever.
  They may name their estates after themselves,
    but they leave their wealth to others.
¹² They will not last long despite their riches—
    they will die like the animals.
¹³ This is the fate of fools,
    though they will be remembered as being so wise.

                                              Interlude

¹⁴ Like sheep, they are led to the grave,
    where death will be their shepherd.
  In the morning the godly will rule over them.
    Their bodies will rot in the grave,
    far from their grand estates.
¹⁵ But as for me, God will redeem my life.
    He will snatch me from the power of death.   *Interlude*

¹⁶ So don't be dismayed when the wicked
grow rich,
and their homes become ever more splendid.
¹⁷ For when they die, they carry nothing with them.
Their wealth will not follow them into the
grave.
¹⁸ In this life they consider themselves fortunate,
and the world loudly applauds their success.
¹⁹ But they will die like all others before them
and never again see the light of day.
²⁰ People who boast of their wealth don't
understand
that they will die like the animals.

Psalm 50

A psalm of Asaph.

¹ The mighty God, the LORD, has spoken;
He has summoned all humanity from east to
west!
² From Mount Zion, the perfection of beauty,
God shines in glorious radiance.
³ Our God approaches with the noise of thunder.
Fire devours everything in His way,
and a great storm rages around Him.

4 Heaven and earth will be His witnesses
   as He judges His people:
5 "Bring My faithful people to Me—
   those who made a covenant with Me by giving
      sacrifices."
6 Then let the heavens proclaim His justice,
   for God Himself will be the judge.   *Interlude*

7 "O My people, listen as I speak.
   Here are My charges against you, O Israel:
   I am God, your God!
8 I have no complaint about your sacrifices
   or the burnt offerings you constantly bring to
      My altar.
9 But I want no more bulls from your barns;
   I want no more goats from your pens.
10 For all the animals of the forest are Mine,
   and I own the cattle on a thousand hills.
11 Every bird of the mountains
   and all the animals of the field belong to Me.
12 If I were hungry, I would not mention it
      to you,
   for all the world is Mine and everything in it.
13 I don't need the bulls you sacrifice;
   I don't need the blood of goats.
14 What I want instead is your true thanks to God;
   I want you to fulfill your vows to the Most High.

[15] Trust Me in your times of trouble,
    and I will rescue you,
    and you will give Me glory."

[16] But God says to the wicked:
    "Recite My laws no longer,
    and don't pretend that you obey Me.
[17] For you refuse My discipline
    and treat My laws like trash.
[18] When you see a thief, you help him,
    and you spend your time with
        adulterers.
[19] Your mouths are filled with
        wickedness,
    and your tongues are full of lies.
[20] You sit around and slander a brother—
    your own mother's son.
[21] While you did all this, I remained silent,
    and you thought I didn't care.
  But now I will rebuke you,
    listing all My charges against you.
[22] Repent, all of you who ignore Me,
    or I will tear you apart,
    and no one will help you.
[23] But giving thanks is a sacrifice that truly honors Me.
    If you keep to My path,
    I will reveal to you the salvation of God."

Proverbs 10

The proverbs of Solomon:

A wise child brings joy to a father; a foolish child brings grief to a mother.

²Ill-gotten gain has no lasting value, but right living can save your life.

³The LORD will not let the godly starve to death, but He refuses to satisfy the craving of the wicked.

⁴Lazy people are soon poor; hard workers get rich.

⁵A wise youth works hard all summer; a youth who sleeps away the hour of opportunity brings shame.

⁶The godly are showered with blessings; evil people cover up their harmful intentions.

⁷We all have happy memories of the godly, but the name of a wicked person rots away.

⁸The wise are glad to be instructed, but babbling fools fall flat on their faces.

⁹People with integrity have firm footing, but those who follow crooked paths will slip and fall.

¹⁰People who wink at wrong cause trouble, but a bold reproof promotes peace.

¹¹The words of the godly lead to life; evil people cover up their harmful intentions.

¹²Hatred stirs up quarrels, but love covers all offenses.

¹³Wise words come from the lips of people with understanding, but fools will be punished with a rod.

[14]Wise people treasure knowledge, but the babbling of a fool invites trouble.

[15]The wealth of the rich is their fortress; the poverty of the poor is their calamity.

[16]The earnings of the godly enhance their lives, but evil people squander their money on sin.

[17]People who accept correction are on the pathway to life, but those who ignore it will lead others astray.

[18]To hide hatred is to be a liar; to slander is to be a fool.

[19]Don't talk too much, for it fosters sin. Be sensible and turn off the flow!

[20]The words of the godly are like sterling silver; the heart of a fool is worthless.

[21]The godly give good advice, but fools are destroyed by their lack of common sense.

[22]The blessing of the LORD makes a person rich, and He adds no sorrow with it.

[23]Doing wrong is fun for a fool, while wise conduct is a pleasure to the wise.

[24]The fears of the wicked will all come true; so will the hopes of the godly.

[25]Disaster strikes like a cyclone, whirling the wicked away, but the godly have a lasting foundation.

[26]Lazy people are a pain to their employer. They are like smoke in the eyes or vinegar that sets the teeth on edge.

[27]Fear of the LORD lengthens one's life, but the years of the wicked are cut short.

²⁸The hopes of the godly result in happiness, but the expectations of the wicked are all in vain.

²⁹The LORD protects the upright but destroys the wicked.

³⁰The godly will never be disturbed, but the wicked will be removed from the land.

³¹The godly person gives wise advice, but the tongue that deceives will be cut off.

³²The godly speak words that are helpful, but the wicked speak only what is corrupt.

Notes

_____

_____

_____

_____

_____

_____

_____

_____

_____

Notes

_____

_____

_____

_____

_____

_____

_____

_____

_____

_____

_____

_____

_____

_____

_____

_____

_____

Psalm 51

For the choir director: A psalm of David, regarding the time Nathan the prophet came to him after David had committed adultery with Bathsheba.

¹ Have mercy on me, O God,
  because of Your unfailing love.
 Because of Your great compassion,
  blot out the stain of my sins.
² Wash me clean from my guilt.
  Purify me from my sin.

³ For I recognize my shameful deeds—
  they haunt me day and night.
⁴ Against You, and You alone, have I sinned;
  I have done what is evil in Your sight.
 You will be proved right in what You say,
  and Your judgment against me is just.

⁵ For I was born a sinner—
  yes, from the moment my mother conceived me.
⁶ But You desire honesty from the heart,
  so You can teach me to be wise in my inmost
   being.

7 Purify me from my sins, and I will be clean;
   wash me, and I will be whiter than snow.
8 Oh, give me back my joy again;
   You have broken me—
   now let me rejoice.
9 Don't keep looking at my sins.
   Remove the stain of my guilt.
10 Create in me a clean heart, O God.
   Renew a right spirit within me.
11 Do not banish me from Your presence,
   and don't take Your Holy Spirit from me.
12 Restore to me again the joy of Your salvation,
   and make me willing to obey You.
13 Then I will teach Your ways to sinners,
   and they will return to You.
14 Forgive me for shedding blood, O God who saves;
   then I will joyfully sing of Your forgiveness.
15 Unseal my lips, O Lord,
   that I may praise You.

16 You would not be pleased with sacrifices,
   or I would bring them.
  If I brought You a burnt offering,
   You would not accept it.
17 The sacrifice You want is a broken spirit.
   A broken and repentant heart, O God,
   You will not despise.

¹⁸ Look with favor on Zion and help her;
     rebuild the walls of Jerusalem.
¹⁹ Then You will be pleased with worthy sacrifices
     and with our whole burnt offerings;
     and bulls will again be sacrificed on Your altar.

Psalm 52

For the choir director: A psalm of David, regarding the time Doeg the Edomite told Saul that Ahimelech had given refuge to David.

¹ You call yourself a hero, do you?
     Why boast about this crime of yours,
     you who have disgraced God's people?
² All day long you plot destruction.
     Your tongue cuts like a sharp razor;
     you're an expert at telling lies.
³ You love evil more than good
     and lies more than truth.   *Interlude*

⁴ You love to say things that harm others,
     you liar!
⁵ But God will strike you down once and for all.
     He will pull you from your home
     and drag you from the land of the living.   *Interlude*

⁶ The righteous will see it and be amazed.
     They will laugh and say,

[7] "Look what happens to mighty warriors
   who do not trust in God.
They trust their wealth instead
   and grow more and more bold in their wickedness."

[8] But I am like an olive tree,
   thriving in the house of God.
I trust in God's unfailing love
   forever and ever.
[9] I will praise You forever, O God,
   for what You have done.
I will wait for Your mercies
   in the presence of Your people.

Psalm 53

For the choir director: A meditation of David.

[1] Only fools say in their hearts,
   "There is no God."
They are corrupt, and their actions are evil;
   no one does good!

[2] God looks down from heaven
   on the entire human race;
He looks to see if there is even one with real
      understanding,
   one who seeks for God.

³ But no, all have turned away from God;
    all have become corrupt.
 No one does good,
    not even one!

⁴ Will those who do evil never learn?
    They eat up my people like bread;
    they wouldn't think of praying to God.
⁵ But then terror will grip them,
    terror like they have never known before.
 God will scatter the bones of your enemies.
    You will put them to shame, for God has rejected them.

⁶ Oh, that salvation would come from Mount Zion to
    rescue Israel!
    For when God restores His people,
    Jacob will shout with joy, and Israel will rejoice.

Psalm 54

For the choir director: A meditation of David, regarding the time the Ziphites came and said to Saul, "We know where David is hiding." To be accompanied by stringed instruments.

¹ Come with great power, O God, and rescue me!
    Defend me with Your might.
² O God, listen to my prayer.
    Pay attention to my plea.

³ For strangers are attacking me;
    violent men are trying to kill me.
    They care nothing for God.   *Interlude*

⁴ But God is my helper.
    The Lord is the One who keeps me alive!
⁵ May my enemies' plans for evil be turned against them.
    Do as You promised and put an end to them.

⁶ I will sacrifice a voluntary offering to You;
    I will praise Your name, O LORD,
    for it is good.
⁷ For You will rescue me from my troubles
    and help me to triumph over my enemies.

Psalm 55

For the choir director: A psalm of David, to be accompanied by stringed instruments.

¹ Listen to my prayer, O God.
    Do not ignore my cry for help!
² Please listen and answer me,
    for I am overwhelmed by my troubles.
³ My enemies shout at me,
    making loud and wicked threats.
  They bring trouble on me,
    hunting me down in their anger.

⁴ My heart is in anguish.
  The terror of death overpowers me.
⁵ Fear and trembling overwhelm me.
  I can't stop shaking.
⁶ Oh, how I wish I had wings like a dove;
  then I would fly away and rest!
⁷ I would fly far away
  to the quiet of the wilderness.   *Interlude*
⁸ How quickly I would escape—
  far away from this wild storm of hatred.

⁹ Destroy them, Lord, and confuse their speech,
  for I see violence and strife in the city.
¹⁰ Its walls are patrolled day and night against
    invaders,
    but the real danger is wickedness within the
    city.
¹¹ Murder and robbery are everywhere there;
  threats and cheating are rampant in the streets.

¹² It is not an enemy who taunts me—
  I could bear that.
  It is not my foes who so arrogantly insult me—
  I could have hidden from them.
¹³ Instead, it is you—my equal,
  my companion and close friend.
¹⁴ What good fellowship we enjoyed
  as we walked together to the house of God.

¹⁵ Let death seize my enemies by surprise;
    let the grave swallow them alive,
    for evil makes its home within them.

¹⁶ But I will call on God,
    and the LORD will rescue me.
¹⁷ Morning, noon, and night
    I plead aloud in my distress,
    and the LORD hears my voice.
¹⁸ He rescues me and keeps me safe
    from the battle waged against me,
    even though many still oppose me.
¹⁹ God, who is king forever,
    will hear me and will humble them.   *Interlude*
 For my enemies refuse to change their
      ways;
    they do not fear God.

²⁰ As for this friend of mine, he betrayed me;
    he broke his promises.
²¹ His words are as smooth as cream,
    but in his heart is war.
 His words are as soothing as lotion,
    but underneath are daggers!

²² Give your burdens to the LORD,
    and He will take care of you.
    He will not permit the godly to slip and fall.

²³ But You, O God, will send the wicked
   down to the pit of destruction.
 Murderers and liars will die young,
   but I am trusting You to save me.

Proverbs 11

The LORD hates cheating, but He delights in honesty.

²Pride leads to disgrace, but with humility comes wisdom.

³Good people are guided by their honesty; treacherous people are destroyed by their dishonesty.

⁴Riches won't help on the day of judgment, but right living is a safeguard against death.

⁵The godly are directed by their honesty; the wicked fall beneath their load of sin.

⁶The godliness of good people rescues them; the ambition of treacherous people traps them.

⁷When the wicked die, their hopes all perish, for they rely on their own feeble strength.

⁸God rescues the godly from danger, but He lets the wicked fall into trouble.

⁹Evil words destroy one's friends; wise discernment rescues the godly.

¹⁰The whole city celebrates when the godly succeed; they shout for joy when the godless die.

¹¹Upright citizens bless a city and make it prosper, but the talk of the wicked tears it apart.

¹²It is foolish to belittle a neighbor; a person with good sense remains silent.

¹³A gossip goes around revealing secrets, but those who are trustworthy can keep a confidence.

¹⁴Without wise leadership, a nation falls; with many counselors, there is safety.

¹⁵Guaranteeing a loan for a stranger is dangerous; it is better to refuse than to suffer later.

¹⁶Beautiful women obtain wealth, and violent men get rich.

¹⁷Your own soul is nourished when you are kind, but you destroy yourself when you are cruel.

¹⁸Evil people get rich for the moment, but the reward of the godly will last.

¹⁹Godly people find life; evil people find death.

²⁰The LORD hates people with twisted hearts, but He delights in those who have integrity.

²¹You can be sure that evil people will be punished, but the children of the godly will go free.

²²A woman who is beautiful but lacks discretion is like a gold ring in a pig's snout.

²³The godly can look forward to happiness, while the wicked can expect only wrath.

²⁴It is possible to give freely and become more wealthy, but those who are stingy will lose everything.

²⁵The generous prosper and are satisfied; those who refresh others will themselves be refreshed.

²⁶People curse those who hold their grain for higher prices, but they bless the one who sells to them in their time of need.

²⁷If you search for good, you will find favor; but if you search for evil, it will find you!

²⁸Trust in your money and down you go! But the godly flourish like leaves in spring.

²⁹Those who bring trouble on their families inherit only the wind. The fool will be a servant to the wise.

³⁰The godly are like trees that bear life-giving fruit, and those who save lives are wise.

³¹If the righteous are rewarded here on earth, how much more true that the wicked and the sinner will get what they deserve!

(ruled note lines, blank)

Notes

_____

_____

_____

_____

_____

_____

_____

_____

_____

_____

_____

_____

_____

_____

_____

_____

_____

_____

_____

_____

_____

Psalm 56

For the choir director: A psalm of David, regarding the time the Philistines seized him in Gath. To be sung to the tune "Dove on Distant Oaks."

¹ O God, have mercy on me.

    The enemy troops press in on me.

    My foes attack me all day long.

² My slanderers hound me constantly,

    and many are boldly attacking me.

³ But when I am afraid,

    I put my trust in You.

⁴ O God, I praise Your word.

    I trust in God, so why should I be afraid?

    What can mere mortals do to me?

⁵ They are always twisting what I say;

    they spend their days plotting ways to harm me.

⁶ They come together to spy on me—

    watching my every step, eager to kill me.

⁷ Don't let them get away with their wickedness;

    in Your anger, O God, throw them to the
       ground.

⁸ You keep track of all my sorrows.
   You have collected all my tears in Your bottle.
   You have recorded each one in Your book.

⁹ On the very day I call to You for help,
   my enemies will retreat.
   This I know: God is on my side.
¹⁰ O God, I praise Your word.
   Yes, LORD, I praise Your word.
¹¹ I trust in God, so why should I be afraid?
   What can mere mortals do to me?

¹² I will fulfill my vows to You, O God,
   and offer a sacrifice of thanks for Your help.
¹³ For You have rescued me from death;
   You have kept my feet from slipping.
 So now I can walk in Your presence, O God,
   in Your life-giving light.

Psalm 57

For the choir director: A psalm of David, regarding the time he fled from Saul and went into the cave. To be sung to the tune "Do Not Destroy!"

¹ Have mercy on me, O God, have mercy!
   I look to You for protection.
 I will hide beneath the shadow of Your wings
   until this violent storm is past.

² I cry out to God Most High,
    to God who will fulfill His purpose for me.
³ He will send help from heaven to save me,
    rescuing me from those who are out to get me.

Interlude

My God will send forth His unfailing love and
    faithfulness.

⁴ I am surrounded by fierce lions
    who greedily devour human prey—
whose teeth pierce like spears and arrows,
    and whose tongues cut like swords.

⁵ Be exalted, O God, above the highest heavens!
    May Your glory shine over all the earth.

⁶ My enemies have set a trap for me.
    I am weary from distress.
They have dug a deep pit in my path,
    but they themselves have fallen into it.   *Interlude*

⁷ My heart is confident in You, O God;
    no wonder I can sing Your praises!
⁸ Wake up, my soul!
    Wake up, O harp and lyre!
    I will waken the dawn with my song.
⁹ I will thank You, Lord, in front of all the
    people.
    I will sing Your praises among the nations.

¹⁰ For Your unfailing love is as high as the heavens.
   Your faithfulness reaches to the clouds.

¹¹ Be exalted, O God, above the highest heavens.
   May Your glory shine over all the earth.

Psalm 58

For the choir director: A psalm of David, to be sung to the tune "Do Not Destroy!"

¹ Justice—do you rulers know the meaning of the word?
   Do you judge the people fairly?
² No, all your dealings are crooked;
   you hand out violence instead of justice.
³ These wicked people are born sinners;
   even from birth they have lied and gone their own
      way.
⁴ They spit poison like deadly snakes;
   they are like cobras that refuse to listen,
⁵ ignoring the tunes of the snake charmers,
   no matter how skillfully they play.

⁶ Break off their fangs, O God!
   Smash the jaws of these lions, O LORD!
⁷ May they disappear like water into thirsty ground.
   Make their weapons useless in their hands.
⁸ May they be like snails that dissolve into slime,

like a stillborn child who will never see the sun.
⁹ God will sweep them away, both young and old,
    faster than a pot heats on an open flame.

¹⁰ The godly will rejoice when they see injustice avenged.
    They will wash their feet in the blood of the wicked.
¹¹ Then at last everyone will say,
    "There truly is a reward for those who live for God;
    surely there is a God who judges justly here on earth."

Psalm 59

For the choir director: A psalm of David, regarding the time Saul sent soldiers to watch David's house in order to kill him. To be sung to the tune "Do Not Destroy!"

¹ Rescue me from my enemies, O God.
    Protect me from those who have come to destroy me.
² Rescue me from these criminals;
    save me from these murderers.

³ They have set an ambush for me.
    Fierce enemies are out there waiting,
    though I have done them no wrong, O LORD.
⁴ Despite my innocence, they prepare to kill me.
    Rise up and help me! Look on my plight!
⁵ O LORD God Almighty, the God of Israel,
    rise up to punish hostile nations.
    Show no mercy to wicked traitors.   *Interlude*

⁶ They come at night,
    snarling like vicious dogs
    as they prowl the streets.
⁷ Listen to the filth that comes from their mouths,
    the piercing swords that fly from their lips.
    "Who can hurt us?" they sneer.

⁸ But LORD, You laugh at them.
    You scoff at all the hostile nations.
⁹ You are my strength; I wait for You to rescue me,
    for You, O God, are my place of safety.
¹⁰ In His unfailing love, my God will come and help me.
    He will let me look down in triumph on all my
        enemies.

¹¹ Don't kill them, for my people soon forget such
        lessons;
    stagger them with Your power, and bring them to
        their knees,
    O Lord our shield.
¹² Because of the sinful things they say,
    because of the evil that is on their lips,
  let them be captured by their pride,
    their curses, and their lies.
¹³ Destroy them in Your anger!
    Wipe them out completely!
  Then the whole world will know
    that God reigns in Israel.   *Interlude*

¹⁴ My enemies come out at night,
    snarling like vicious dogs
    as they prowl the streets.
¹⁵ They scavenge for food
    but go to sleep unsatisfied.

¹⁶ But as for me, I will sing about Your power.
    I will shout with joy each morning because of Your
        unfailing love.
  For You have been my refuge,
    a place of safety in the day of distress.

¹⁷ O my Strength, to You I sing praises,
    for You, O God, are my refuge,
    the God who shows me unfailing love.

Psalm 60

For the choir director: A psalm of David useful for teaching, regarding the time David fought Aram-naharaim and Aram-zobah, and Joab returned and killed twelve thousand Edomites in the Valley of Salt. To be sung to the tune "Lily of the Testimony."

¹ You have rejected us, O God, and broken our defenses.
    You have been angry with us; now restore us to Your
        favor.
² You have shaken our land and split it open.
    Seal the cracks before it completely collapses.

³ You have been very hard on us,
  making us drink wine that sent us reeling.
⁴ But You have raised a banner for those who
      honor You—
  a rallying point in the face of attack.   *Interlude*

⁵ Use Your strong right arm to save us,
  and rescue Your beloved people.
⁶ God has promised this by His holiness:
  "I will divide up Shechem with joy.
  I will measure out the valley of Succoth.
⁷ Gilead is Mine,
  and Manasseh is Mine.
Ephraim will produce My warriors,
  and Judah will produce My kings.
⁸ Moab will become My lowly servant,
  and Edom will be My slave.
  I will shout in triumph over the Philistines."

⁹ But who will bring me into the fortified city?
  Who will bring me victory over Edom?
¹⁰ Have You rejected us, O God?
  Will You no longer march with our armies?
¹¹ Oh, please help us against our enemies,
  for all human help is useless.
¹² With God's help we will do mighty things,
  for He will trample down our foes.

Proverbs 12

To learn, you must love discipline; it is stupid to hate correction.

²The LORD approves of those who are good, but He condemns those who plan wickedness.

³Wickedness never brings stability; only the godly have deep roots.

⁴A worthy wife is her husband's joy and crown; a shameful wife saps his strength.

⁵The plans of the godly are just; the advice of the wicked is treacherous.

⁶The words of the wicked are like a murderous ambush, but the words of the godly save lives.

⁷The wicked perish and are gone, but the children of the godly stand firm.

⁸Everyone admires a person with good sense, but a warped mind is despised.

⁹It is better to be a nobody with a servant than to be self-important but have no food.

¹⁰The godly are concerned for the welfare of their animals, but even the kindness of the wicked is cruel.

¹¹Hard work means prosperity; only fools idle away their time.

¹²Thieves are jealous of each other's loot, while the godly bear their own fruit.

13The wicked are trapped by their own words, but the godly escape such trouble.

14People can get many good things by the words they say; the work of their hands also gives them many benefits.

15Fools think they need no advice, but the wise listen to others.

16A fool is quick-tempered, but a wise person stays calm when insulted.

17An honest witness tells the truth; a false witness tells lies.

18Some people make cutting remarks, but the words of the wise bring healing.

19Truth stands the test of time; lies are soon exposed.

20Deceit fills hearts that are plotting evil; joy fills hearts that are planning peace!

21No real harm befalls the godly, but the wicked have their fill of trouble.

22The LORD hates those who don't keep their word, but He delights in those who do.

23Wise people don't make a show of their knowledge, but fools broadcast their folly.

24Work hard and become a leader; be lazy and become a slave.

25Worry weighs a person down; an encouraging word cheers a person up.

26The godly give good advice to their friends; the wicked lead them astray.

²⁷Lazy people don't even cook the game they catch, but the diligent make use of everything they find.

²⁸The way of the godly leads to life; their path does not lead to death.

Notes

_____

_____

_____

_____

_____

_____

_____

_____

_____

_____

_____

_____

Notes

_____

_____

_____

_____

_____

_____

_____

_____

_____

_____

_____

_____

_____

_____

_____

_____

_____

_____

_____

_____

_____

Psalm 61

For the choir director: A psalm of David, to be accompanied by stringed instruments.

¹ O God, listen to my cry!
    Hear my prayer!
² From the ends of the earth,
    I will cry to You for help,
    for my heart is overwhelmed.
  Lead me to the towering rock of safety,
³   for You are my safe refuge,
    a fortress where my enemies cannot reach
        me.
⁴ Let me live forever in Your sanctuary,
    safe beneath the shelter of Your wings!   *Interlude*

⁵ For You have heard my vows, O God.
    You have given me an inheritance reserved for those
        who fear Your name.

⁶ Add many years to the life of the king!
    May his years span the generations!
⁷ May he reign under God's protection forever.
    Appoint Your unfailing love and faithfulness to watch
        over him.

⁸ Then I will always sing praises to Your name
    as I fulfill my vows day after day.

Psalm 62

For Jeduthun, the choir director: A psalm of David.

¹ I wait quietly before God,
    for my salvation comes from Him.
² He alone is my rock and my salvation,
    my fortress where I will never be shaken.

³ So many enemies against one man—
    all of them trying to kill me.
  To them I'm just a broken-down wall
    or a tottering fence.
⁴ They plan to topple me from my high position.
    They delight in telling lies about me.
  They are friendly to my face,
    but they curse me in their hearts.   *Interlude*

⁵ I wait quietly before God,
    for my hope is in Him.
⁶ He alone is my rock and my salvation,
    my fortress where I will not be shaken.
⁷ My salvation and my honor come from God alone.
    He is my refuge, a rock where no enemy can reach me.

⁸ O my people, trust in Him at all times.
　　Pour out your heart to Him,
　　　for God is our refuge.   *Interlude*

⁹ From the greatest to the lowliest—
　　all are nothing in His sight.
　If you weigh them on the scales,
　　they are lighter than a puff of air.
¹⁰ Don't try to get rich
　　by extortion or robbery.
　And if your wealth increases,
　　don't make it the center of your life.

¹¹ God has spoken plainly,
　　and I have heard it many times:
　Power, O God, belongs to You;
¹²　unfailing love, O Lord, is Yours.
　Surely You judge all people
　　according to what they have done.

Psalm 63

A psalm of David, regarding a time when David was in the wilderness of Judah.

¹ O God, You are my God;
　　I earnestly search for You.
　My soul thirsts for You;
　　my whole body longs for You

in this parched and weary land
   where there is no water.

² I have seen You in Your sanctuary
   and gazed upon Your power and glory.
³ Your unfailing love is better to me than life
     itself;
   how I praise You!
⁴ I will honor You as long as I live,
   lifting up my hands to You in prayer.
⁵ You satisfy me more than the richest of foods.
   I will praise You with songs of joy.

⁶ I lie awake thinking of You,
   meditating on You through the night.
⁷ I think how much You have helped me;
   I sing for joy in the shadow of Your protecting
     wings.
⁸ I follow close behind You;
   Your strong right hand holds me securely.

⁹ But those plotting to destroy me will come to ruin.
   They will go down into the depths of the earth.
¹⁰ They will die by the sword
   and become the food of jackals.

¹¹ But the king will rejoice in God.
   All who trust in Him will praise Him,
   while liars will be silenced.

Psalm 64

For the choir director: A psalm of David.

¹ O God, listen to my complaint.
    Do not let my enemies' threats overwhelm me.
² Protect me from the plots of the wicked,
    from the scheming of those who do evil.
³ Sharp tongues are the swords they wield;
    bitter words are the arrows they aim.
⁴ They shoot from ambush at the innocent,
    attacking suddenly and fearlessly.
⁵ They encourage each other to do evil
    and plan how to set their traps.
    "Who will ever notice?" they ask.
⁶ As they plot their crimes, they say,
    "We have devised the perfect plan!"
    Yes, the human heart and mind are cunning.

⁷ But God Himself will shoot them down.
    Suddenly, His arrows will pierce them.
⁸ Their own words will be turned against them, destroying
    them.
    All who see it happening will shake their heads in
    scorn.
⁹ Then everyone will stand in awe,
    proclaiming the mighty acts of God,
    realizing all the amazing things He does.

¹⁰ The godly will rejoice in the LORD
    and find shelter in Him.
  And those who do what is right
    will praise Him.

Psalm 65

For the choir director: A psalm of David. A song.

¹ What mighty praise, O God,
    belongs to You in Zion.
  We will fulfill our vows to You,
²   for You answer our prayers,
    and to You all people will come.
³ Though our hearts are filled with sins,
    You forgive them all.
⁴ What joy for those You choose to bring near,
    those who live in Your holy courts.
  What joys await us
    inside Your holy Temple.

⁵ You faithfully answer our prayers with awesome deeds,
    O God our savior.
  You are the hope of everyone on earth,
    even those who sail on distant seas.
⁶ You formed the mountains by Your power
    and armed Yourself with mighty strength.

⁷ You quieted the raging oceans
      with their pounding waves
      and silenced the shouting of the
            nations.
⁸ Those who live at the ends of the earth
      stand in awe of Your wonders.
   From where the sun rises to where it sets,
      You inspire shouts of joy.

⁹ You take care of the earth and water it,
      making it rich and fertile.
   The rivers of God will not run dry;
      they provide a bountiful harvest of grain,
      for You have ordered it so.
¹⁰ You drench the plowed ground with rain,
      melting the clods and leveling the ridges.
   You soften the earth with showers
      and bless its abundant crops.
¹¹ You crown the year with a bountiful harvest;
      even the hard pathways overflow with
            abundance.
¹² The wilderness becomes a lush pasture,
      and the hillsides blossom with joy.
¹³ The meadows are clothed with flocks of
            sheep,
      and the valleys are carpeted with grain.
      They all shout and sing for joy!

Proverbs 13

A wise child accepts a parent's discipline; a young mocker refuses to listen.

²Good people enjoy the positive results of their words, but those who are treacherous crave violence.

³Those who control their tongue will have a long life; a quick retort can ruin everything.

⁴Lazy people want much but get little, but those who work hard will prosper and be satisfied.

⁵Those who are godly hate lies; the wicked come to shame and disgrace.

⁶Godliness helps people all through life, while the evil are destroyed by their wickedness.

⁷Some who are poor pretend to be rich; others who are rich pretend to be poor.

⁸The rich can pay a ransom, but the poor won't even get threatened.

⁹The life of the godly is full of light and joy, but the sinner's light is snuffed out.

¹⁰Pride leads to arguments; those who take advice are wise.

¹¹Wealth from get-rich-quick schemes quickly disappears; wealth from hard work grows.

¹²Hope deferred makes the heart sick, but when dreams come true, there is life and joy.

¹³People who despise advice will find themselves in trouble; those who respect it will succeed.

¹⁴The advice of the wise is like a life-giving fountain; those who accept it avoid the snares of death.

¹⁵A person with good sense is respected; a treacherous person walks a rocky road.

¹⁶Wise people think before they act; fools don't and even brag about it!

¹⁷An unreliable messenger stumbles into trouble, but a reliable messenger brings healing.

¹⁸If you ignore criticism, you will end in poverty and disgrace; if you accept criticism, you will be honored.

¹⁹It is pleasant to see dreams come true, but fools will not turn from evil to attain them.

²⁰Whoever walks with the wise will become wise; whoever walks with fools will suffer harm.

²¹Trouble chases sinners, while blessings chase the righteous!

²²Good people leave an inheritance to their grandchildren, but the sinner's wealth passes to the godly.

²³A poor person's farm may produce much food, but injustice sweeps it all away.

²⁴If you refuse to discipline your children, it proves you don't love them; if you love your children, you will be prompt to discipline them.

²⁵The godly eat to their hearts' content, but the belly of the wicked goes hungry.

Notes

Psalm 66

For the choir director: A psalm. A song.

¹ Shout joyful praises to God, all the earth!
²   Sing about the glory of His name!
    Tell the world how glorious He is.
³ Say to God, "How awesome are Your deeds!
    Your enemies cringe before Your mighty power.
⁴ Everything on earth will worship You;
    they will sing Your praises,
    shouting Your name in glorious songs."   *Interlude*

⁵ Come and see what our God has done,
    what awesome miracles He does for His people!
⁶ He made a dry path through the Red Sea,
    and His people went across on foot.
    Come, let us rejoice in who He is.
⁷ For by His great power He rules forever.
    He watches every movement of the nations;
    let no rebel rise in defiance.   *Interlude*

⁸ Let the whole world bless our God
    and sing aloud His praises.

⁹ Our lives are in His hands,
    and He keeps our feet from stumbling.
¹⁰ You have tested us, O God;
    You have purified us like silver melted in a crucible.
¹¹ You captured us in Your net
    and laid the burden of slavery on our backs.
¹² You sent troops to ride across our broken bodies.
    We went through fire and flood.
    But You brought us to a place of great abundance.

¹³ Now I come to Your Temple with burnt offerings
    to fulfill the vows I made to You—
¹⁴ yes, the sacred vows You heard me make
    when I was in deep trouble.
¹⁵ That is why I am sacrificing burnt offerings to You—
    the best of my rams as a pleasing aroma.
    And I will sacrifice bulls and goats.   *Interlude*

¹⁶ Come and listen, all you who fear God,
    and I will tell you what He did for me.
¹⁷ For I cried out to Him for help,
    praising Him as I spoke.
¹⁸ If I had not confessed the sin in my heart,
    my Lord would not have listened.
¹⁹ But God did listen!
    He paid attention to my prayer.

²⁰ Praise God, who did not ignore my prayer
    and did not withdraw His unfailing love from me.

Psalm 67

For the choir director: A psalm, to be accompanied by stringed instruments. A song.

¹ May God be merciful and bless us.
　　May His face shine with favor upon us.   *Interlude*
² May Your ways be known throughout the earth,
　　Your saving power among people everywhere.
³ May the nations praise You, O God.
　　Yes, may all the nations praise You.

⁴ How glad the nations will be, singing for joy,
　　because You govern them with justice
　　and direct the actions of the whole world.   *Interlude*
⁵ May the nations praise You, O God.
　　Yes, may all the nations praise You.

⁶ Then the earth will yield its harvests,
　　and God, our God, will richly bless us.
⁷ Yes, God will bless us,
　　and people all over the world will fear Him.

Psalm 68

For the choir director: A psalm of David. A song.

¹ Arise, O God, and scatter Your enemies.
　　Let those who hate God run for their lives.

² Drive them off like smoke blown by the wind.
    Melt them like wax in fire.
    Let the wicked perish in the presence of God.
³ But let the godly rejoice.
    Let them be glad in God's presence.
    Let them be filled with joy.

⁴ Sing praises to God and to His name!
    Sing loud praises to Him who rides the clouds.
  His name is the LORD—
    rejoice in His presence!

⁵ Father to the fatherless, defender of widows—
    this is God, whose dwelling is holy.
⁶ God places the lonely in families;
    He sets the prisoners free and gives them joy.
    But for rebels, there is only famine and distress.

⁷ O God, when You led Your people from Egypt,
    when You marched through the wilderness,

Interlude

⁸ the earth trembled, and the heavens poured
        rain
    before You, the God of Sinai,
    before God, the God of Israel.
⁹ You sent abundant rain, O God,
    to refresh the weary Promised Land.
¹⁰ There Your people finally settled,

and with a bountiful harvest, O God,
You provided for Your needy people.

[11] The Lord announces victory,
and throngs of women shout the happy news.
[12] Enemy kings and their armies flee,
while the women of Israel divide the plunder.
[13] Though they lived among the sheepfolds,
now they are covered with silver and gold,
as a dove is covered by its wings.
[14] The Almighty scattered the enemy kings
like a blowing snowstorm on Mount Zalmon.

[15] The majestic mountains of Bashan
stretch high into the sky.
[16] Why do you look with envy, O rugged mountains,
at Mount Zion, where God has chosen to live,
where the LORD Himself will live forever?

[17] Surrounded by unnumbered thousands of chariots,
the Lord came from Mount Sinai into His sanctuary.
[18] When You ascended to the heights,
You led a crowd of captives.
You received gifts from the people,
even from those who rebelled against You.
Now the LORD God will live among us here.

[19] Praise the Lord; praise God our savior!
For each day He carries us in His arms.   *Interlude*

²⁰ Our God is a God who saves!
>   The Sovereign LORD rescues us from death.

²¹ But God will smash the heads of His enemies,
>   crushing the skulls of those who love their guilty
>   ways.
²² The Lord says, "I will bring My enemies down from
>   Bashan;
>   I will bring them up from the depths of the sea.
²³ You, My people, will wash your feet in their blood,
>   and even your dogs will get their share!"

²⁴ Your procession has come into view, O God—
>   the procession of my God and King
>   as He goes into the sanctuary.
²⁵ Singers are in front, musicians are behind;
>   with them are young women playing tambourines.
²⁶ Praise God, all you people of Israel;
>   praise the LORD, the source of Israel's life.
²⁷ Look, the little tribe of Benjamin leads the way.
>   Then comes a great throng of rulers from Judah
>   and all the rulers of Zebulun and Naphtali.

²⁸ Summon Your might, O God.
>   Display Your power, O God, as You have in the
>   past.
²⁹ The kings of the earth are bringing tribute
>   to Your Temple in Jerusalem.

³⁰ Rebuke these enemy nations—
    these wild animals lurking in the reeds,
    this herd of bulls among the weaker calves.
  Humble those who demand tribute from us.
    Scatter the nations that delight in war.
³¹ Let Egypt come with gifts of precious metals;
    let Ethiopia bow in submission to God.
³² Sing to God, you kingdoms of the earth.
    Sing praises to the Lord.   *Interlude*

³³ Sing to the One who rides across the ancient heavens,
    His mighty voice thundering from the sky.
³⁴ Tell everyone about God's power.
    His majesty shines down on Israel;
    His strength is mighty in the heavens.
³⁵ God is awesome in His sanctuary.
    The God of Israel gives power and strength to His
      people.

  Praise be to God!

Psalm 69

For the choir director: A psalm of David, to be sung to the tune "Lilies."

¹ Save me, O God,
    for the floodwaters are up to my neck.

² Deeper and deeper I sink into the mire;
    I can't find a foothold to stand on.
  I am in deep water,
    and the floods overwhelm me.
³ I am exhausted from crying for help;
    my throat is parched and dry.
  My eyes are swollen with weeping,
    waiting for my God to help me.

⁴ Those who hate me without cause
    are more numerous than the hairs on my
        head.
  These enemies who seek to destroy me
    are doing so without cause.
  They attack me with lies,
    demanding that I give back what I didn't steal.

⁵ O God, You know how foolish I am;
    my sins cannot be hidden from You.
⁶ Don't let those who trust in You stumble because
        of me,
    O Sovereign LORD Almighty.
  Don't let me cause them to be humiliated,
    O God of Israel.
⁷ For I am mocked and shamed for Your sake;
    humiliation is written all over my face.
⁸ Even my own brothers pretend they don't know me;
    they treat me like a stranger.

⁹ Passion for Your house burns within me,
   so those who insult You are also insulting me.
¹⁰ When I weep and fast before the LORD,
   they scoff at me.
¹¹ When I dress in sackcloth to show sorrow,
   they make fun of me.
¹² I am the favorite topic of town gossip,
   and all the drunkards sing about me.

¹³ But I keep right on praying to You, LORD,
   hoping this is the time You will show me
      favor.
   In Your unfailing love, O God,
   answer my prayer with Your sure salvation.
¹⁴ Pull me out of the mud;
   don't let me sink any deeper!
   Rescue me from those who hate me,
   and pull me from these deep waters.
¹⁵ Don't let the floods overwhelm me,
   or the deep waters swallow me,
   or the pit of death devour me.

¹⁶ Answer my prayers, O LORD,
   for Your unfailing love is wonderful.
   Turn and take care of me,
   for Your mercy is so plentiful.
¹⁷ Don't hide from Your servant;
   answer me quickly, for I am in deep trouble!

¹⁸ Come and rescue me;
    free me from all my enemies.

¹⁹ You know the insults I endure—
    the humiliation and disgrace.
  You have seen all my enemies
    and know what they have said.
²⁰ Their insults have broken my heart,
    and I am in despair.
  If only one person would show some pity;
    if only one would turn and comfort me.
²¹ But instead, they give me poison for food;
    they offer me sour wine to satisfy my thirst.

²² Let the bountiful table set before them become
        a snare,
    and let their security become a trap.
²³ Let their eyes go blind so they cannot see,
    and let their bodies grow weaker and weaker.
²⁴ Pour out Your fury on them;
    consume them with Your burning anger.
²⁵ May their homes become desolate
    and their tents be deserted.
²⁶ To those You have punished, they add insult to
        injury;
    they scoff at the pain of those You have hurt.
²⁷ Pile their sins up high,
    and don't let them go free.

²⁸ Erase their names from the Book of Life;
     don't let them be counted among the righteous.

²⁹ I am suffering and in pain.
     Rescue me, O God, by Your saving power.

³⁰ Then I will praise God's name with singing,
     and I will honor Him with thanksgiving.
³¹ For this will please the LORD more than sacrificing
     an ox
     or presenting a bull with its horns and
     hooves.
³² The humble will see their God at work and be
     glad.
     Let all who seek God's help live in joy.
³³ For the LORD hears the cries of His needy ones;
     He does not despise His people who are
     oppressed.

³⁴ Praise Him, O heaven and earth,
     the seas and all that move in them.
³⁵ For God will save Jerusalem
     and rebuild the towns of Judah.
  His people will live there
     and take possession of the land.
³⁶ The descendants of those who obey Him will inherit the
     land,
     and those who love Him will live there in safety.

Psalm 70

For the choir director: A psalm of David, to bring us to the LORD's remembrance.

¹ Please, God, rescue me!
    Come quickly, LORD, and help me.
² May those who try to destroy me
    be humiliated and put to shame.
  May those who take delight in my trouble
    be turned back in disgrace.
³ Let them be horrified by their shame,
    for they said, "Aha! We've got him now!"
⁴ But may all who search for You
    be filled with joy and gladness.
  May those who love Your salvation
    repeatedly shout, "God is great!"
⁵ But I am poor and needy;
    please hurry to my aid, O God.
  You are my helper and my savior;
    O LORD, do not delay!

Proverbs 14

A wise woman builds her house; a foolish woman tears
hers down with her own hands.

   ²Those who follow the right path fear the LORD; those
who take the wrong path despise Him.

³The talk of fools is a rod for their backs, but the words of the wise keep them out of trouble.

⁴An empty stable stays clean, but no income comes from an empty stable.

⁵A truthful witness does not lie; a false witness breathes lies.

⁶A mocker seeks wisdom and never finds it, but knowledge comes easily to those with understanding.

⁷Stay away from fools, for you won't find knowledge there.

⁸The wise look ahead to see what is coming, but fools deceive themselves.

⁹Fools make fun of guilt, but the godly acknowledge it and seek reconciliation.

¹⁰Each heart knows its own bitterness, and no one else can fully share its joy.

¹¹The house of the wicked will perish, but the tent of the godly will flourish.

¹²There is a path before each person that seems right, but it ends in death.

¹³Laughter can conceal a heavy heart; when the laughter ends, the grief remains.

¹⁴Backsliders get what they deserve; good people receive their reward.

¹⁵Only simpletons believe everything they are told! The prudent carefully consider their steps.

¹⁶The wise are cautious and avoid danger; fools plunge ahead with great confidence.

¹⁷Those who are short-tempered do foolish things, and schemers are hated.

¹⁸The simpleton is clothed with folly, but the wise person is crowned with knowledge.

¹⁹Evil people will bow before good people; the wicked will bow at the gates of the godly.

²⁰The poor are despised even by their neighbors, while the rich have many "friends."

²¹It is sin to despise one's neighbors; blessed are those who help the poor.

²²If you plot evil, you will be lost; but if you plan good, you will be granted unfailing love and faithfulness.

²³Work brings profit, but mere talk leads to poverty!

²⁴Wealth is a crown for the wise; the effort of fools yields only folly.

²⁵A truthful witness saves lives, but a false witness is a traitor.

²⁶Those who fear the LORD are secure; He will be a place of refuge for their children.

²⁷Fear of the LORD is a life-giving fountain; it offers escape from the snares of death.

²⁸A growing population is a king's glory; a dwindling nation is his doom.

²⁹Those who control their anger have great understanding; those with a hasty temper will make mistakes.

³⁰A relaxed attitude lengthens life; jealousy rots it away.

³¹Those who oppress the poor insult their Maker, but those who help the poor honor Him.

³²The wicked are crushed by their sins, but the godly have a refuge when they die.

³³Wisdom is enshrined in an understanding heart; wisdom is not found among fools.

³⁴Godliness exalts a nation, but sin is a disgrace to any people.

³⁵A king rejoices in servants who know what they are doing; he is angry with those who cause trouble.

Notes

_____

_____

_____

_____

_____

_____

_____

_____

_____

_____

_____

_____

_____

_____

_____

_____

_____

_____

_____

_____

_____

_____

_____

_____

_____

_____

_____

_____

Psalm 71

¹ O LORD, You are my refuge;
   never let me be disgraced.
² Rescue me! Save me from my enemies, for You are just.
   Turn Your ear to listen and set me free.
³ Be to me a protecting rock of safety,
   where I am always welcome.
 Give the order to save me,
   for You are my rock and my fortress.

⁴ My God, rescue me from the power of the wicked,
   from the clutches of cruel oppressors.
⁵ O Lord, You alone are my hope.
   I've trusted You, O LORD, from childhood.
⁶ Yes, You have been with me from birth;
   from my mother's womb You have cared for me.
 No wonder I am always praising You!

⁷ My life is an example to many,
   because You have been my strength and protection.
⁸ That is why I can never stop praising You;
   I declare Your glory all day long.

⁹ And now, in my old age, don't set me aside.

   Don't abandon me when my strength is failing.

¹⁰ For my enemies are whispering against me.

   They are plotting together to kill me.

¹¹ They say, "God has abandoned him.

   Let's go and get him,

   for there is no one to help him now."

¹² O God, don't stay away.

   My God, please hurry to help me.

¹³ Bring disgrace and destruction on those who

      accuse me.

   May humiliation and shame cover

   those who want to harm me.

¹⁴ But I will keep on hoping for You to help me;

   I will praise You more and more.

¹⁵ I will tell everyone about Your righteousness.

   All day long I will proclaim Your saving power,

   for I am overwhelmed by how much You have done

      for me.

¹⁶ I will praise Your mighty deeds, O Sovereign LORD.

   I will tell everyone that You alone are just and good.

¹⁷ O God, You have taught me from my earliest

      childhood,

   and I have constantly told others about the

      wonderful things You do.

¹⁸ Now that I am old and gray,
    do not abandon me, O God.
  Let me proclaim Your power to this new
      generation,
    Your mighty miracles to all who come after me.

¹⁹ Your righteousness, O God, reaches to the highest
      heavens.
    You have done such wonderful things.
    Who can compare with You, O God?
²⁰ You have allowed me to suffer much hardship,
    but You will restore me to life again
    and lift me up from the depths of the earth.
²¹ You will restore me to even greater honor
    and comfort me once again.

²² Then I will praise You with music on the harp,
    because You are faithful to Your promises,
      O God.
  I will sing for You with a lyre,
    O Holy One of Israel.
²³ I will shout for joy and sing Your praises,
    for You have redeemed me.
²⁴ I will tell about Your righteous deeds
    all day long,
  for everyone who tried to hurt me
    has been shamed and humiliated.

Psalm 72

A psalm of Solomon.

¹ Give justice to the king, O God,
   and righteousness to the king's Son.
² Help Him judge Your people in the right way;
   let the poor always be treated fairly.
³ May the mountains yield prosperity for all,
   and may the hills be fruitful,
   because the king does what is right.
⁴ Help Him to defend the poor,
   to rescue the children of the needy,
   and to crush their oppressors.
⁵ May He live as long as the sun shines,
   as long as the moon continues in the skies.
   Yes, forever!
⁶ May His reign be as refreshing as the springtime rains—
   like the showers that water the earth.
⁷ May all the godly flourish during His reign.
   May there be abundant prosperity until the end of time.

⁸ May He reign from sea to sea,
   and from the Euphrates River to the ends of the earth.
⁹ Desert nomads will bow before Him;
   His enemies will fall before Him in the dust.
¹⁰ The western kings of Tarshish and the islands
   will bring Him tribute.

The eastern kings of Sheba and Seba
   will bring Him gifts.
¹¹ All kings will bow before Him,
   and all nations will serve Him.

¹² He will rescue the poor when they cry to Him;
   He will help the oppressed, who have no one to defend
      them.
¹³ He feels pity for the weak and the needy,
   and He will rescue them.
¹⁴ He will save them from oppression and from
      violence,
   for their lives are precious to Him.

¹⁵ Long live the King!
   May the gold of Sheba be given to Him.
  May the people always pray for Him
   and bless Him all day long.
¹⁶ May there be abundant crops throughout the
      land,
   flourishing even on the mountaintops.
  May the fruit trees flourish as they do in Lebanon,
   sprouting up like grass in a field.
¹⁷ May the King's name endure forever;
   may it continue as long as the sun shines.
  May all nations be blessed through Him
   and bring Him praise.

¹⁸ Bless the LORD God, the God of Israel,
　　who alone does such wonderful things.
¹⁹ Bless His glorious name forever!
　　Let the whole earth be filled with His glory.
　　Amen and amen!

²⁰ (This ends the prayers of David son of Jesse.)

Psalm 73

A psalm of Asaph.

¹ Truly God is good to Israel,
　　to those whose hearts are pure.

² But as for me, I came so close to the edge of the cliff!
　　My feet were slipping, and I was almost gone.
³ For I envied the proud
　　when I saw them prosper despite their wickedness.
⁴ They seem to live such a painless life;
　　their bodies are so healthy and strong.
⁵ They aren't troubled like other people
　　or plagued with problems like everyone else.
⁶ They wear pride like a jeweled necklace,
　　and their clothing is woven of cruelty.
⁷ These fat cats have everything
　　their hearts could ever wish for!

⁸ They scoff and speak only evil;
   in their pride they seek to crush others.
⁹ They boast against the very heavens,
   and their words strut throughout the earth.
¹⁰ And so the people are dismayed and confused,
   drinking in all their words.
¹¹ "Does God realize what is going on?" they ask.
   "Is the Most High even aware of what is
      happening?"
¹² Look at these arrogant people—
   enjoying a life of ease while their riches
      multiply.

¹³ Was it for nothing that I kept my heart pure
   and kept myself from doing wrong?
¹⁴ All I get is trouble all day long;
   every morning brings me pain.

¹⁵ If I had really spoken this way,
   I would have been a traitor to Your people.
¹⁶ So I tried to understand why the wicked prosper.
   But what a difficult task it is!
¹⁷ Then one day I went into Your sanctuary, O God,
   and I thought about the destiny of the wicked.
¹⁸ Truly, You put them on a slippery path
   and send them sliding over the cliff to destruction.
¹⁹ In an instant they are destroyed,
   swept away by terrors.

²⁰ Their present life is only a dream
    that is gone when they awake.
  When You arise, O Lord,
    You will make them vanish from this life.

²¹ Then I realized how bitter I had become,
    how pained I had been by all I had seen.
²² I was so foolish and ignorant—
    I must have seemed like a senseless animal
      to You.
²³ Yet I still belong to You;
    You are holding my right hand.
²⁴ You will keep on guiding me with Your counsel,
    leading me to a glorious destiny.
²⁵ Whom have I in heaven but You?
    I desire You more than anything on earth.
²⁶ My health may fail, and my spirit may grow
      weak,
    but God remains the strength of my heart;
    He is mine forever.

²⁷ But those who desert Him will perish,
    for You destroy those who abandon You.
²⁸ But as for me, how good it is to be near God!
    I have made the Sovereign LORD my shelter,
    and I will tell everyone about the wonderful things
      You do.

Psalm 74

A psalm of Asaph.

¹ O God, why have You rejected us forever?
  Why is Your anger so intense against the sheep of Your
    own pasture?
² Remember that we are the people You chose in ancient
    times,
  the tribe You redeemed as Your own special
    possession!
  And remember Jerusalem, Your home here
    on earth.
³ Walk through the awful ruins of the city;
  see how the enemy has destroyed Your sanctuary.
⁴ There Your enemies shouted their victorious battle
    cries;
  there they set up their battle standards.
⁵ They chopped down the entrance
  like woodcutters in a forest.
⁶ With axes and picks,
  they smashed the carved paneling.
⁷ They set the sanctuary on fire, burning it to the ground.
  They utterly defiled the place that bears Your holy
    name.
⁸ Then they thought, "Let's destroy everything!"
  So they burned down all the places where God was
    worshiped.

⁹ We see no miraculous signs
  as evidence that You will save us.
 All the prophets are gone;
  no one can tell us when it will end.
¹⁰ How long, O God, will You allow our enemies to mock
    You?
  Will You let them dishonor Your name forever?
¹¹ Why do You hold back Your strong right hand?
  Unleash Your powerful fist and deliver a deathblow.

¹² You, O God, are my king from ages past,
  bringing salvation to the earth.
¹³ You split the sea by Your strength
  and smashed the sea monster's heads.
¹⁴ You crushed the heads of Leviathan
  and let the desert animals eat him.
¹⁵ You caused the springs and streams to gush forth,
  and You dried up rivers that never run dry.
¹⁶ Both day and night belong to You;
  You made the starlight and the sun.
¹⁷ You set the boundaries of the earth,
  and You make both summer and winter.

¹⁸ See how these enemies scoff at You, LORD.
  A foolish nation has dishonored Your name.
¹⁹ Don't let these wild beasts destroy Your doves.
  Don't forget Your afflicted people forever.

²⁰ Remember Your covenant promises,
    for the land is full of darkness and violence!
²¹ Don't let the downtrodden be constantly disgraced!
    Instead, let these poor and needy ones give praise to
        Your name.

²² Arise, O God, and defend Your cause.
    Remember how these fools insult You all day long.
²³ Don't overlook these things Your enemies have said.
    Their uproar of rebellion grows ever louder.

Psalm 75

For the choir director: A psalm of Asaph, to be sung to the tune "Do Not Destroy!"
A song.

¹ We thank You, O God!
    We give thanks because You are near.
    People everywhere tell of Your mighty miracles.

² God says, "At the time I have planned,
    I will bring justice against the wicked.
³ When the earth quakes and its people live in turmoil,
    I am the One who keeps its foundations firm.

                                                        Interlude

⁴ "I warned the proud, 'Stop your boasting!'
    I told the wicked, 'Don't raise your fists!

5 Don't lift your fists in defiance at the heavens
  or speak with rebellious arrogance.'"

6 For no one on earth—from east or west,
  or even from the wilderness—
  can raise another person up.
7 It is God alone who judges;
  He decides who will rise and who will fall.
8 For the LORD holds a cup in His hand;
  it is full of foaming wine mixed with spices.
He pours the wine out in judgment,
  and all the wicked must drink it,
  draining it to the dregs.

9 But as for me, I will always proclaim what God has done;
  I will sing praises to the God of Israel.

10 For God says, "I will cut off the strength of the
   wicked,
   but I will increase the power of the godly."

Proverbs 15

A gentle answer turns away wrath, but harsh words stir up anger.

2 The wise person makes learning a joy; fools spout only foolishness.

³The LORD is watching everywhere, keeping His eye on both the evil and the good.

⁴Gentle words bring life and health; a deceitful tongue crushes the spirit.

⁵Only a fool despises a parent's discipline; whoever learns from correction is wise.

⁶There is treasure in the house of the godly, but the earnings of the wicked bring trouble.

⁷Only the wise can give good advice; fools cannot do so.

⁸The LORD hates the sacrifice of the wicked, but He delights in the prayers of the upright.

⁹The LORD despises the way of the wicked, but He loves those who pursue godliness.

¹⁰Whoever abandons the right path will be severely punished; whoever hates correction will die.

¹¹Even the depths of Death and Destruction are known by the LORD. How much more does He know the human heart!

¹²Mockers don't love those who rebuke them, so they stay away from the wise.

¹³A glad heart makes a happy face; a broken heart crushes the spirit.

¹⁴A wise person is hungry for truth, while the fool feeds on trash.

¹⁵For the poor, every day brings trouble; for the happy heart, life is a continual feast.

¹⁶It is better to have little with fear for the LORD than to have great treasure with turmoil.

¹⁷A bowl of soup with someone you love is better than steak with someone you hate.

¹⁸A hothead starts fights; a cool-tempered person tries to stop them.

¹⁹A lazy person has trouble all through life; the path of the upright is easy!

²⁰Sensible children bring joy to their father; foolish children despise their mother.

²¹Foolishness brings joy to those who have no sense; a sensible person stays on the right path.

²²Plans go wrong for lack of advice; many counselors bring success.

²³Everyone enjoys a fitting reply; it is wonderful to say the right thing at the right time!

²⁴The path of the wise leads to life above; they leave the grave behind.

²⁵The LORD destroys the house of the proud, but He protects the property of widows.

²⁶The LORD despises the thoughts of the wicked, but He delights in pure words.

²⁷Dishonest money brings grief to the whole family, but those who hate bribes will live.

²⁸The godly think before speaking; the wicked spout evil words.

²⁹The LORD is far from the wicked, but He hears the prayers of the righteous.

³⁰A cheerful look brings joy to the heart; good news makes for good health.

³¹If you listen to constructive criticism, you will be at home among the wise.

³²If you reject criticism, you only harm yourself; but if you listen to correction, you grow in understanding.

³³Fear of the LORD teaches a person to be wise; humility precedes honor.

Notes

_____

_____

_____

_____

_____

_____

_____

_____

_____

Psalm 76

*For the choir director: A psalm of Asaph, to be accompanied by stringed instruments.
A song.*

¹ God is well known in Judah;
   His name is great in Israel.
² Jerusalem is where He lives;
   Mount Zion is His home.
³ There He breaks the arrows of the enemy,
   the shields and swords and weapons of His foes.

Interlude

⁴ You are glorious and more majestic
   than the everlasting mountains.
⁵ The mightiest of our enemies have been plundered.
   They lie before us in the sleep of death.
   No warrior could lift a hand against us.
⁶ When You rebuked them, O God of Jacob,
   their horses and chariots stood still.

⁷ No wonder You are greatly feared!
   Who can stand before You when Your anger explodes?
⁸ From heaven You sentenced Your enemies;
   the earth trembled and stood silent before You.

⁹ You stand up to judge those who do evil, O God,
  and to rescue the oppressed of the earth.   *Interlude*

¹⁰ Human opposition only enhances Your glory,
  for You use it as a sword of judgment.

¹¹ Make vows to the LORD your God, and fulfill them.
  Let everyone bring tribute to the Awesome One.
¹² For He breaks the spirit of princes
  and is feared by the kings of the earth.

Psalm 77

For Jeduthun, the choir director: A psalm of Asaph.

¹ I cry out to God without holding back.
  Oh, that God would listen to me!
² When I was in deep trouble,
  I searched for the Lord.
  All night long I pray, with hands lifted toward heaven,
    pleading.
  There can be no joy for me until He acts.
³ I think of God, and I moan,
  overwhelmed with longing for His help.   *Interlude*

⁴ You don't let me sleep.
  I am too distressed even to pray!
⁵ I think of the good old days, long since ended,

⁶ when my nights were filled with joyful
      songs.
   I search my soul and think about the difference
      now.
⁷ Has the Lord rejected me forever?
   Will He never again show me favor?
⁸ Is His unfailing love gone forever?
   Have His promises permanently failed?
⁹ Has God forgotten to be kind?
   Has He slammed the door on His compassion?

Interlude

¹⁰ And I said, "This is my fate,
      that the blessings of the Most High have changed to
      hatred."
¹¹ I recall all You have done, O LORD;
   I remember Your wonderful deeds of long ago.
¹² They are constantly in my thoughts.
   I cannot stop thinking about them.

¹³ O God, Your ways are holy.
   Is there any god as mighty as You?
¹⁴ You are the God of miracles and wonders!
   You demonstrate Your awesome power among the
      nations.
¹⁵ You have redeemed Your people by Your strength,
   the descendants of Jacob and of Joseph by Your might.

Interlude

¹⁶ When the Red Sea saw You, O God,
    its waters looked and trembled!
    The sea quaked to its very depths.
¹⁷ The clouds poured down their rain;
    the thunder rolled and crackled in the sky.
    Your arrows of lightning flashed.
¹⁸ Your thunder roared from the whirlwind;
    the lightning lit up the world!
    The earth trembled and shook.
¹⁹ Your road led through the sea,
    Your pathway through the mighty waters—
    a pathway no one knew was there!
²⁰ You led Your people along that road like a flock
        of sheep,
    with Moses and Aaron as their shepherds.

Psalm 78

A psalm of Asaph.

¹ O my people, listen to my teaching.
    Open your ears to what I am saying,
²   for I will speak to you in a parable.
  I will teach you hidden lessons from our past—
³   stories we have heard and know,
    stories our ancestors handed down to us.

⁴ We will not hide these truths from our
      children
    but will tell the next generation about the glorious
      deeds of the LORD.
    We will tell of His power and the mighty miracles
      He did.
⁵ For He issued His decree to Jacob;
    He gave His law to Israel.
  He commanded our ancestors
    to teach them to their children,
⁶ so the next generation might know them—
    even the children not yet born—
    that they in turn might teach their
      children.
⁷ So each generation can set its hope anew
      on God,
    remembering His glorious miracles
    and obeying His commands.
⁸ Then they will not be like their ancestors—
    stubborn, rebellious, and unfaithful,
    refusing to give their hearts to God.

⁹ The warriors of Ephraim, though fully armed,
    turned their backs and fled when the day of battle
      came.
¹⁰ They did not keep God's covenant,
    and they refused to live by His law.

¹¹ They forgot what He had done—
    the wonderful miracles He had shown them,
¹²   the miracles He did for their ancestors in Egypt, on the
    plain of Zoan.
¹³ For He divided the sea before them and led them
    through!
    The water stood up like walls beside them!
¹⁴ In the daytime He led them by a cloud,
    and at night by a pillar of fire.
¹⁵ He split open the rocks in the wilderness
    to give them plenty of water, as from a gushing spring.
¹⁶ He made streams pour from the rock,
    making the waters flow down like a river!

¹⁷ Yet they kept on with their sin,
    rebelling against the Most High in the desert.
¹⁸ They willfully tested God in their hearts,
    demanding the foods they craved.
¹⁹ They even spoke against God Himself, saying,
    "God can't give us food in the desert.
²⁰ Yes, He can strike a rock so water gushes out,
    but He can't give His people bread and meat."
²¹ When the LORD heard them, He was angry.
    The fire of His wrath burned against Jacob.
  Yes, His anger rose against Israel,
²²   for they did not believe God
    or trust Him to care for them.

23 But He commanded the skies to open—
   He opened the doors of heaven—
24   and rained down manna for them to eat.
   He gave them bread from heaven.
25   They ate the food of angels!
   God gave them all they could hold.
26 He released the east wind in the heavens
   and guided the south wind by His mighty power.
27 He rained down meat as thick as dust—
   birds as plentiful as the sands along the seashore!
28 He caused the birds to fall within their camp
   and all around their tents.
29 The people ate their fill.
   He gave them what they wanted.
30 But before they finished eating this food they had craved,
   while the meat was yet in their mouths,
31 the anger of God rose against them,
   and He killed their strongest men;
   He struck down the finest of Israel's young men.
32 But in spite of this, the people kept on sinning.
   They refused to believe in His miracles.
33 So He ended their lives in failure
   and gave them years of terror.

34 When God killed some of them, the rest finally sought
   Him.
   They repented and turned to God.

³⁵ Then they remembered that God was their rock,
    that their Redeemer was the Most High.
³⁶ But they followed Him only with their words;
    they lied to Him with their tongues.
³⁷ Their hearts were not loyal to Him.
    They did not keep His covenant.
³⁸ Yet He was merciful and forgave their sins
    and didn't destroy them all.
  Many a time He held back His anger
    and did not unleash His fury!
³⁹ For He remembered that they were merely mortal,
    gone in a moment like a breath of wind, never to return.

⁴⁰ Oh, how often they rebelled against Him in the desert
    and grieved His heart in the wilderness.
⁴¹ Again and again they tested God's patience
    and frustrated the Holy One of Israel.
⁴² They forgot about His power
    and how He rescued them from their enemies.
⁴³ They forgot His miraculous signs in Egypt,
    His wonders on the plain of Zoan.
⁴⁴ For He turned their rivers into blood,
    so no one could drink from the streams.
⁴⁵ He sent vast swarms of flies to consume them
    and hordes of frogs to ruin them.
⁴⁶ He gave their crops to caterpillars;
    their harvest was consumed by locusts.

⁴⁷ He destroyed their grapevines with hail
    and shattered their sycamores with sleet.
⁴⁸ He abandoned their cattle to the hail,
    their livestock to bolts of lightning.
⁴⁹ He loosed on them His fierce anger—
    all His fury, rage, and hostility.
  He dispatched against them
    a band of destroying angels.
⁵⁰ He turned His anger against them;
    He did not spare the Egyptians' lives
    but handed them over to the plague.
⁵¹ He killed the oldest son in each Egyptian family,
    the flower of youth throughout the land of Egypt.
⁵² But He led His own people like a flock of sheep,
    guiding them safely through the wilderness.
⁵³ He kept them safe so they were not afraid;
    but the sea closed in upon their enemies.
⁵⁴ He brought them to the border of His holy land,
    to this land of hills He had won for them.
⁵⁵ He drove out the nations before them;
    He gave them their inheritance by lot.
  He settled the tribes of Israel into their homes.

⁵⁶ Yet though He did all this for them,
    they continued to test His patience.
  They rebelled against the Most High
    and refused to follow His decrees.

⁵⁷ They turned back and were as faithless as their parents
        had been.

      They were as useless as a crooked bow.
⁵⁸ They made God angry by building altars to other gods;
      they made Him jealous with their idols.
⁵⁹ When God heard them, He was very angry,
      and He rejected Israel completely.
⁶⁰ Then He abandoned His dwelling at Shiloh,
      the Tabernacle where He had lived among the people.
⁶¹ He allowed the Ark of His might to be captured;
      He surrendered His glory into enemy hands.
⁶² He gave His people over to be butchered by the sword,
      because He was so angry with His own people—His
        special possession.
⁶³ Their young men were killed by fire;
      their young women died before singing their wedding
        songs.
⁶⁴ Their priests were slaughtered,
      and their widows could not mourn their deaths.
⁶⁵ Then the Lord rose up as though waking from sleep,
      like a mighty man aroused from a drunken stupor.
⁶⁶ He routed His enemies
      and sent them to eternal shame.
⁶⁷ But He rejected Joseph's descendants;
      He did not choose the tribe of Ephraim.
⁶⁸ He chose instead the tribe of Judah,
      Mount Zion, which He loved.

⁶⁹ There He built His towering sanctuary,
     as solid and enduring as the earth itself.
⁷⁰ He chose His servant David,
     calling him from the sheep pens.
⁷¹ He took David from tending the ewes and lambs
     and made him the shepherd of Jacob's descendants—
     God's own people, Israel.
⁷² He cared for them with a true heart
     and led them with skillful hands.

Psalm 79

A psalm of Asaph.

¹ O God, pagan nations have conquered Your land, Your
     special possession.
     They have defiled Your holy Temple
     and made Jerusalem a heap of ruins.
² They have left the bodies of Your servants
     as food for the birds of heaven.
   The flesh of Your godly ones
     has become food for the wild animals.
³ Blood has flowed like water all around Jerusalem;
     no one is left to bury the dead.
⁴ We are mocked by our neighbors,
     an object of scorn and derision to those around us.

⁵ O LORD, how long will You be angry with us? Forever?
How long will Your jealousy burn like fire?
⁶ Pour out Your wrath on the nations that refuse to
    recognize You—
on kingdoms that do not call upon Your name.
⁷ For they have devoured Your people Israel,
making the land a desolate wilderness.
⁸ Oh, do not hold us guilty for our former sins!
Let Your tenderhearted mercies quickly meet our needs,
for we are brought low to the dust.
⁹ Help us, O God of our salvation!
Help us for the honor of Your name.
Oh, save us and forgive our sins
for the sake of Your name.
¹⁰ Why should pagan nations be allowed to scoff,
asking, "Where is their God?"
Show us Your vengeance against the nations,
for they have spilled the blood of Your servants.
¹¹ Listen to the moaning of the prisoners.
Demonstrate Your great power by saving those
    condemned to die.

¹² O Lord, take sevenfold vengeance on our neighbors
for the scorn they have hurled at You.
¹³ Then we Your people, the sheep of Your pasture,
will thank You forever and ever,
praising Your greatness from generation to generation.

Proverbs 16

We can gather our thoughts, but the LORD gives the right answer.

²People may be pure in their own eyes, but the LORD examines their motives.

³Commit your work to the LORD, and then your plans will succeed.

⁴The LORD has made everything for His own purposes, even the wicked for punishment.

⁵The LORD despises pride; be assured that the proud will be punished.

⁶Unfailing love and faithfulness cover sin; evil is avoided by fear of the LORD.

⁷When the ways of people please the LORD, He makes even their enemies live at peace with them.

⁸It is better to be poor and godly than rich and dishonest.

⁹We can make our plans, but the LORD determines our steps.

¹⁰The king speaks with divine wisdom; He must never judge unfairly.

¹¹The LORD demands fairness in every business deal; He sets the standard.

¹²A king despises wrongdoing, for his rule depends on his justice.

¹³The king is pleased with righteous lips; he loves those who speak honestly.

[14]The anger of the king is a deadly threat; the wise do what they can to appease it.

[15]When the king smiles, there is life; his favor refreshes like a gentle rain.

[16]How much better to get wisdom than gold, and understanding than silver!

[17]The path of the upright leads away from evil; whoever follows that path is safe.

[18]Pride goes before destruction, and haughtiness before a fall.

[19]It is better to live humbly with the poor than to share plunder with the proud.

[20]Those who listen to instruction will prosper; those who trust the LORD will be happy.

[21]The wise are known for their understanding, and instruction is appreciated if it's well presented.

[22]Discretion is a life-giving fountain to those who possess it, but discipline is wasted on fools.

[23]From a wise mind comes wise speech; the words of the wise are persuasive.

[24]Kind words are like honey—sweet to the soul and healthy for the body.

[25]There is a path before each person that seems right, but it ends in death.

[26]It is good for workers to have an appetite; an empty stomach drives them on.

[27]Scoundrels hunt for scandal; their words are a destructive blaze.

[28]A troublemaker plants seeds of strife; gossip separates the best of friends.

[29]Violent people deceive their companions, leading them down a harmful path.

[30]With narrowed eyes, they plot evil; without a word, they plan their mischief.

[31]Gray hair is a crown of glory; it is gained by living a godly life.

[32]It is better to be patient than powerful; it is better to have self-control than to conquer a city.

[33]We may throw the dice, but the LORD determines how they fall.

Notes

_____

_____

_____

_____

_____

_____

_____

_____

_____

_____

_____

_____

_____

_____

_____

_____

_____

_____

_____

Psalm 80

For the choir director: A psalm of Asaph, to be sung to the tune "Lilies of the Covenant."

¹ Please listen, O Shepherd of Israel,
   You who lead Israel like a flock.
  O God, enthroned above the cherubim,
   display Your radiant glory
²   to Ephraim, Benjamin, and Manasseh.
  Show us Your mighty power.
   Come to rescue us!

³ Turn us again to Yourself, O God.
   Make Your face shine down upon us.
   Only then will we be saved.

⁴ O LORD God Almighty,
   how long will You be angry and reject our
      prayers?
⁵ You have fed us with sorrow
   and made us drink tears by the bucketful.
⁶ You have made us the scorn of neighboring nations.
   Our enemies treat us as a joke.

⁷ Turn us again to Yourself, O God Almighty.

Make Your face shine down upon us.

Only then will we be saved.

⁸ You brought us from Egypt as though we were a tender
vine;

You drove away the pagan nations and transplanted
us into Your land.

⁹ You cleared the ground for us,

and we took root and filled the land.

¹⁰ The mountains were covered with our shade;

the mighty cedars were covered with our branches.

¹¹ We spread our branches west to the Mediterranean Sea,

our limbs east to the Euphrates River.

¹² But now, why have You broken down our walls

so that all who pass may steal our fruit?

¹³ The boar from the forest devours us,

and the wild animals feed on us.

¹⁴ Come back, we beg You, O God Almighty.

Look down from heaven and see our plight.

Watch over and care for this vine

¹⁵   that You Yourself have planted,

this son You have raised for Yourself.

¹⁶ For we are chopped up and burned by our enemies.

May they perish at the sight of Your frown.

¹⁷ Strengthen the man You love,

the son of Your choice.

¹⁸ Then we will never forsake You again.
   Revive us so we can call on Your name once more.

¹⁹ Turn us again to Yourself, O LORD God Almighty.
   Make Your face shine down upon us.
   Only then will we be saved.

Psalm 81

For the choir director: A psalm of Asaph, to be accompanied by a stringed instrument.

¹ Sing praises to God, our strength.
   Sing to the God of Israel.
² Sing! Beat the tambourine.
   Play the sweet lyre and the harp.
³ Sound the trumpet for a sacred feast
   when the moon is new,
   when the moon is full.
⁴ For this is required by the laws of Israel;
   it is a law of the God of Jacob.
⁵ He made it a decree for Israel
   when He attacked Egypt to set us free.

   I heard an unknown voice that said,
⁶ "Now I will relieve your shoulder of its burden;
   I will free your hands from their heavy tasks.

⁷ You cried to Me in trouble, and I saved you;
   I answered out of the thundercloud.
  I tested your faith at Meribah,
     when you complained that there was no water.

Interlude

⁸ "Listen to Me, O My people, while I give you stern
     warnings.
   O Israel, if you would only listen!
⁹ You must never have a foreign god;
     you must not bow down before a false god.
¹⁰ For it was I, the LORD your God,
     who rescued you from the land of Egypt.
     Open your mouth wide, and I will fill it with good
        things.

¹¹ "But no, My people wouldn't listen.
   Israel did not want Me around.
¹² So I let them follow their blind and stubborn way,
     living according to their own desires.
¹³ But oh, that My people would listen to Me!
   Oh, that Israel would follow Me, walking in My paths!
¹⁴ How quickly I would then subdue their enemies!
   How soon My hands would be upon their foes!
¹⁵ Those who hate the LORD would cringe before Him;
     their desolation would last forever.
¹⁶ But I would feed you with the best of foods.
   I would satisfy you with wild honey from the rock."

Psalm 82

A psalm of Asaph.

¹ God presides over heaven's court;
    He pronounces judgment on the judges:
² "How long will you judges hand down unjust
      decisions?
    How long will you shower special favors on the
      wicked?   *Interlude*

³ "Give fair judgment to the poor and the orphan;
    uphold the rights of the oppressed and the
      destitute.
⁴ Rescue the poor and helpless;
    deliver them from the grasp of evil people.
⁵ But these oppressors know nothing;
    they are so ignorant!
  And because they are in darkness,
    the whole world is shaken to the core.
⁶ I say, 'You are gods
    and children of the Most High.
⁷ But in death you are mere men.
    You will fall as any prince,
    for all must die.'"

⁸ Rise up, O God, and judge the earth,
    for all the nations belong to You.

Psalm 83

A psalm of Asaph. A song.

¹ O God, don't sit idly by,
   silent and inactive!
² Don't You hear the tumult of Your enemies?
   Don't You see what Your arrogant enemies are
      doing?
³ They devise crafty schemes against Your people,
   laying plans against Your precious ones.
⁴ "Come," they say, "let us wipe out Israel as a
      nation.
   We will destroy the very memory of its existence."
⁵   This was their unanimous decision.
   They signed a treaty as allies against You—
⁶   these Edomites and Ishmaelites,
   Moabites and Hagrites,
⁷   Gebalites, Ammonites, and Amalekites,
   and people from Philistia and Tyre.
⁸ Assyria has joined them, too,
   and is allied with the descendants of Lot.   *Interlude*

⁹ Do to them as You did to the Midianites
   or as You did to Sisera and Jabin at the Kishon
      River.
¹⁰ They were destroyed at Endor,
   and their decaying corpses fertilized the soil.

¹¹ Let their mighty nobles die as Oreb and Zeeb did.
   - Let all their princes die like Zebah and Zalmunna,
¹² for they said, "Let us seize for our own use
   these pasturelands of God!"

¹³ O my God, blow them away like whirling dust,
   like chaff before the wind!
¹⁴ As a fire roars through a forest
   and as a flame sets mountains ablaze,
¹⁵ chase them with Your fierce storms;
   terrify them with Your tempests.
¹⁶ Utterly disgrace them
   until they submit to Your name, O LORD.
¹⁷ Let them be ashamed and terrified forever.
   Make them failures in everything they do,
¹⁸ until they learn that You alone are called the LORD,
   that You alone are the Most High, supreme over all
      the earth.

Psalm 84

For the choir director: A psalm of the descendants of Korah, to be accompanied by a stringed instrument.

¹ How lovely is Your dwelling place,
   O LORD Almighty.
² I long, yes, I faint with longing
   to enter the courts of the LORD.

With my whole being, body and soul,
 I will shout joyfully to the living God.
³ Even the sparrow finds a home there,
 and the swallow builds her nest
 and raises her young—
 at a place near Your altar,
 O LORD Almighty, my King and my God!
⁴ How happy are those who can live in Your house,
 always singing Your praises.   *Interlude*

⁵ Happy are those who are strong in the LORD,
 who set their minds on a pilgrimage to Jerusalem.
⁶ When they walk through the Valley of Weeping,
 it will become a place of refreshing springs,
 where pools of blessing collect after the rains!
⁷ They will continue to grow stronger,
 and each of them will appear before God in Jerusalem.

⁸ O LORD God Almighty, hear my prayer.
 Listen, O God of Israel.   *Interlude*

⁹ O God, look with favor upon the king, our
   protector!
 Have mercy on the one You have anointed.

¹⁰ A single day in Your courts
 is better than a thousand anywhere else!
 I would rather be a gatekeeper in the house of my God
 than live the good life in the homes of the wicked.

¹¹ For the LORD God is our light and protector.

He gives us grace and glory.

No good thing will the LORD withhold

from those who do what is right.

¹² O LORD Almighty,

happy are those who trust in You.

Psalm 85

For the choir director: A psalm of the descendants of Korah.

¹ LORD, You have poured out amazing blessings on Your
land!

You have restored the fortunes of Israel.

² You have forgiven the guilt of Your people—

yes, You have covered all their sins.   *Interlude*

³ You have withdrawn Your fury.

You have ended Your blazing anger.

⁴ Now turn to us again, O God of our salvation.

Put aside Your anger against us.

⁵ Will You be angry with us always?

Will You prolong Your wrath to distant generations?

⁶ Won't You revive us again,

so Your people can rejoice in You?

⁷ Show us Your unfailing love, O LORD,

and grant us Your salvation.

⁸ I listen carefully to what God the LORD is saying,
    for He speaks peace to His people, His faithful ones.
    But let them not return to their foolish ways.
⁹ Surely His salvation is near to those who honor
    Him;
    our land will be filled with His glory.

¹⁰ Unfailing love and truth have met together.
    Righteousness and peace have kissed!
¹¹ Truth springs up from the earth,
    and righteousness smiles down from heaven.
¹² Yes, the LORD pours down His blessings.
    Our land will yield its bountiful crops.
¹³ Righteousness goes as a herald before Him,
    preparing the way for His steps.

Proverbs 17

A dry crust eaten in peace is better than a great feast with
strife.

²A wise slave will rule over the master's shameful sons
and will share their inheritance.

³Fire tests the purity of silver and gold, but the LORD
tests the heart.

⁴Wrongdoers listen to wicked talk; liars pay attention to
destructive words.

⁵Those who mock the poor insult their Maker; those who rejoice at the misfortune of others will be punished.

⁶Grandchildren are the crowning glory of the aged; parents are the pride of their children.

⁷Eloquent speech is not fitting for a fool; even less are lies fitting for a ruler.

⁸A bribe seems to work like magic for those who give it; they succeed in all they do.

⁹Disregarding another person's faults preserves love; telling about them separates close friends.

¹⁰A single rebuke does more for a person of understanding than a hundred lashes on the back of a fool.

¹¹Evil people seek rebellion, but they will be severely punished.

¹²It is safer to meet a bear robbed of her cubs than to confront a fool caught in folly.

¹³If you repay evil for good, evil will never leave your house.

¹⁴Beginning a quarrel is like opening a floodgate, so drop the matter before a dispute breaks out.

¹⁵The LORD despises those who acquit the guilty and condemn the innocent.

¹⁶It is senseless to pay tuition to educate a fool who has no heart for wisdom.

¹⁷A friend is always loyal, and a brother is born to help in time of need.

¹⁸It is poor judgment to co-sign a friend's note, to become responsible for a neighbor's debts.

¹⁹Anyone who loves to quarrel loves sin; anyone who speaks boastfully invites disaster.

²⁰The crooked heart will not prosper; the twisted tongue tumbles into trouble.

²¹It is painful to be the parent of a fool; there is no joy for the father of a rebel.

²²A cheerful heart is good medicine, but a broken spirit saps a person's strength.

²³The wicked accept secret bribes to pervert justice.

²⁴Sensible people keep their eyes glued on wisdom, but a fool's eyes wander to the ends of the earth.

²⁵A foolish child brings grief to a father and bitterness to a mother.

²⁶It is wrong to fine the godly for being good or to punish nobles for being honest!

²⁷A truly wise person uses few words; a person with understanding is even-tempered.

²⁸Even fools are thought to be wise when they keep silent; when they keep their mouths shut, they seem intelligent.

Notes

Psalm 86

A prayer of David.

¹ Bend down, O LORD, and hear my prayer;
  answer me, for I need Your help.
² Protect me, for I am devoted to You.
  Save me, for I serve You and trust You.
  You are my God.
³ Be merciful, O Lord,
  for I am calling on You constantly.
⁴ Give me happiness, O Lord,
  for my life depends on You.
⁵ O Lord, You are so good, so ready to forgive,
  so full of unfailing love for all who ask Your
    aid.
⁶ Listen closely to my prayer, O LORD;
  hear my urgent cry.
⁷ I will call to You whenever trouble strikes,
  and You will answer me.

⁸ Nowhere among the pagan gods is there a god like You,
    O Lord.
  There are no other miracles like Yours.

⁹ All the nations—and You made each one—
   will come and bow before You, Lord;
   they will praise Your great and holy name.
¹⁰ For You are great and perform great miracles.
   You alone are God.

¹¹ Teach me Your ways, O LORD,
   that I may live according to Your truth!
  Grant me purity of heart,
   that I may honor You.
¹² With all my heart I will praise You, O Lord
      my God.
   I will give glory to Your name forever,
¹³ for Your love for me is very great.
   You have rescued me from the depths of death!

¹⁴ O God, insolent people rise up against me;
   violent people are trying to kill me.
   And You mean nothing to them.
¹⁵ But You, O Lord, are a merciful and gracious God,
   slow to get angry,
   full of unfailing love and truth.
¹⁶ Look down and have mercy on me.
   Give strength to Your servant;
   yes, save me, for I am Your servant.
¹⁷ Send me a sign of Your favor.
   Then those who hate me will be put to shame,
   for You, O LORD, help and comfort me.

Psalm 87

A psalm of the descendants of Korah. A song.

¹ On the holy mountain stands the city founded
        by the LORD.
²   He loves the city of Jerusalem
     more than any other city in Israel.
³ O city of God,
        what glorious things are said of You!   *Interlude*

⁴ I will record Egypt and Babylon among those
        who know Me—
     also Philistia and Tyre, and even distant
        Ethiopia.
     They have all become citizens of
        Jerusalem!
⁵ And it will be said of Jerusalem,
        "Everyone has become a citizen
        here."
     And the Most High will personally bless
        this city.
⁶ When the LORD registers the nations,
     He will say, "This one has become a citizen
        of Jerusalem."   *Interlude*

⁷ At all the festivals, the people will
        sing,
     "The source of my life is in Jerusalem!"

Psalm 88

For the choir director: A psalm of the descendants of Korah, to be sung to the tune
"The Suffering of Affliction." A psalm of Heman the Ezrahite. A song.

¹ O LORD, God of my salvation,
    I have cried out to You day and night.
² Now hear my prayer;
    listen to my cry.
³ For my life is full of troubles,
    and death draws near.
⁴ I have been dismissed as one who is dead,
    like a strong man with no strength left.
⁵ They have abandoned me to death,
    and I am as good as dead.
  I am forgotten,
    cut off from Your care.
⁶ You have thrust me down to the lowest pit,
    into the darkest depths.
⁷ Your anger lies heavy on me;
    wave after wave engulfs me.   *Interlude*

⁸ You have caused my friends to loathe me;
    You have sent them all away.
  I am in a trap with no way of escape.
⁹   My eyes are blinded by my tears.
  Each day I beg for Your help, O LORD;
    I lift my pleading hands to You for mercy.

¹⁰ Of what use to the dead are Your miracles?

Do the dead get up and praise You?   *Interlude*

¹¹ Can those in the grave declare Your
            unfailing love?

    In the place of destruction, can they
        proclaim Your faithfulness?

¹² Can the darkness speak of Your miracles?

    Can anyone in the land of forgetfulness talk about
        Your righteousness?

¹³ O LORD, I cry out to You.

    I will keep on pleading day by day.

¹⁴ O LORD, why do You reject me?

    Why do You turn Your face away from me?

¹⁵ I have been sickly and close to death since
        my youth.

    I stand helpless and desperate before
        Your terrors.

¹⁶ Your fierce anger has overwhelmed me.

    Your terrors have cut me off.

¹⁷ They swirl around me like floodwaters all
        day long.

    They have encircled me completely.

¹⁸ You have taken away my companions and
        loved ones;

    only darkness remains.

Psalm 89

A psalm of Ethan the Ezrahite.

¹ I will sing of the tender mercies of the LORD forever!
   Young and old will hear of Your faithfulness.
² Your unfailing love will last forever.
   Your faithfulness is as enduring as the heavens.

³ The LORD said, "I have made a solemn agreement with
      David, My chosen servant.
   I have sworn this oath to him:
⁴ 'I will establish your descendants as kings forever;
   they will sit on your throne from now until eternity.'"

Interlude

⁵ All heaven will praise Your miracles, LORD;
   myriads of angels will praise You for Your faithfulness.
⁶ For who in all of heaven can compare with the LORD?
   What mightiest angel is anything like the LORD?
⁷ The highest angelic powers stand in awe of God.
   He is far more awesome than those who surround His
      throne.
⁸ O LORD God Almighty!
   Where is there anyone as mighty as You, LORD?
   Faithfulness is Your very character.

⁹ You are the One who rules the oceans.
   When their waves rise in fearful storms, You subdue
      them.

¹⁰ You are the One who crushed the great sea monster.
> You scattered Your enemies with Your mighty arm.

¹¹ The heavens are Yours, and the earth is Yours;
> everything in the world is Yours—You created it all.

¹² You created north and south.
> Mount Tabor and Mount Hermon praise Your name.

¹³ Powerful is Your arm!
> Strong is Your hand!
> Your right hand is lifted high in glorious strength.

¹⁴ Your throne is founded on two strong pillars—
> righteousness and justice.
> Unfailing love and truth walk before You as
> attendants.

¹⁵ Happy are those who hear the joyful call to worship,
> for they will walk in the light of Your presence, LORD.

¹⁶ They rejoice all day long in Your wonderful reputation.
> They exult in Your righteousness.

¹⁷ You are their glorious strength.
> Our power is based on Your favor.

¹⁸ Yes, our protection comes from the LORD,
> and He, the Holy One of Israel, has given us
> our king.

¹⁹ You once spoke in a vision to Your prophet and said,
> "I have given help to a warrior.
> I have selected him from the common people to be
> king.

234

²⁰ I have found My servant David.
   I have anointed him with My holy oil.
²¹ I will steady him,
   and I will make him strong.
²² His enemies will not get the best of him,
   nor will the wicked overpower him.
²³ I will beat down his adversaries before him
   and destroy those who hate him.
²⁴ My faithfulness and unfailing love will be with him,
   and he will rise to power because of Me.
²⁵ I will extend his rule from the Mediterranean Sea in
      the west
   to the Tigris and Euphrates rivers in the east.
²⁶ And he will say to Me, 'You are my Father,
   my God, and the Rock of My salvation.'
²⁷ I will make him My firstborn son,
   the mightiest king on earth.
²⁸ I will love him and be kind to him forever;
   My covenant with him will never end.
²⁹ I will preserve an heir for him;
   his throne will be as endless as the days of heaven.
³⁰ But if his sons forsake My law
   and fail to walk in My ways,
³¹ if they do not obey My decrees
   and fail to keep My commands,
³² then I will punish their sin with the rod,
   and their disobedience with beating.

³³ But I will never stop loving him,
    nor let My promise to him fail.
³⁴ No, I will not break My covenant;
    I will not take back a single word I said.
³⁵ I have sworn an oath to David,
    and in My holiness I cannot lie:
³⁶ His dynasty will go on forever;
    his throne is as secure as the sun,
³⁷   as eternal as the moon,
    My faithful witness in the sky!"   *Interlude*

³⁸ But now You have rejected him.
    Why are You so angry with the one You chose as king?
³⁹ You have renounced Your covenant with him,
    for You have thrown his crown in the dust.
⁴⁰ You have broken down the walls protecting him
    and laid in ruins every fort defending him.
⁴¹ Everyone who comes along has robbed him
    while his neighbors mock.
⁴² You have strengthened his enemies against him
    and made them all rejoice.
⁴³ You have made his sword useless
    and have refused to help him in battle.
⁴⁴ You have ended his splendor
    and overturned his throne.
⁴⁵ You have made him old before his time
    and publicly disgraced him.   *Interlude*

⁴⁶ O LORD, how long will this go on?
  Will You hide Yourself forever?
  How long will Your anger burn like fire?
⁴⁷ Remember how short my life is,
  how empty and futile this human existence!
⁴⁸ No one can live forever; all will die.
  No one can escape the power of the grave.   *Interlude*

⁴⁹ Lord, where is Your unfailing love?
  You promised it to David with a faithful pledge.
⁵⁰ Consider, Lord, how Your servants are disgraced!
  I carry in my heart the insults of so many people.
⁵¹ Your enemies have mocked me, O LORD;
  they mock the one You anointed as king.

⁵² Blessed be the LORD forever!
  Amen and amen!

Psalm 90

A prayer of Moses, the man of God.

¹ Lord, through all the generations
  You have been our home!
² Before the mountains were created,
  before You made the earth and the world,
  You are God, without beginning or end.

³ You turn people back to dust, saying,
    "Return to dust!"
⁴ For You, a thousand years are as yesterday!
    They are like a few hours!
⁵ You sweep people away like dreams that disappear
    or like grass that springs up in the morning.
⁶ In the morning it blooms and flourishes,
    but by evening it is dry and withered.
⁷ We wither beneath Your anger;
    we are overwhelmed by Your fury.
⁸ You spread out our sins before You—
    our secret sins—and You see them all.
⁹ We live our lives beneath Your wrath.
    We end our lives with a groan.

¹⁰ Seventy years are given to us!
    Some may even reach eighty.
  But even the best of these years are filled with pain and
        trouble;
    soon they disappear, and we are gone.
¹¹ Who can comprehend the power of Your anger?
    Your wrath is as awesome as the fear You deserve.
¹² Teach us to make the most of our time,
    so that we may grow in wisdom.

¹³ O LORD, come back to us!
    How long will You delay?
    Take pity on Your servants!

¹⁴ Satisfy us in the morning with Your unfailing love,
  so we may sing for joy to the end of our lives.
¹⁵ Give us gladness in proportion to our former misery!
  Replace the evil years with good.
¹⁶ Let us see Your miracles again;
  let our children see Your glory at work.
¹⁷ And may the Lord our God show us His approval
  and make our efforts successful.
  Yes, make our efforts successful!

Proverbs 18

A recluse is self-indulgent, snarling at every sound princi-
ple of conduct.

²Fools have no interest in understanding; they only want
to air their own opinions.

³When the wicked arrive, contempt, shame, and
disgrace are sure to follow.

⁴A person's words can be life-giving water; words of true
wisdom are as refreshing as a bubbling brook.

⁵It is wrong for a judge to favor the guilty or condemn
the innocent.

⁶Fools get into constant quarrels; they are asking for a
beating.

⁷The mouths of fools are their ruin; their lips get them
into trouble.

⁸What dainty morsels rumors are—but they sink deep into one's heart.

⁹A lazy person is as bad as someone who destroys things.

¹⁰The name of the LORD is a strong fortress; the godly run to Him and are safe.

¹¹The rich think of their wealth as an impregnable defense; they imagine it is a high wall of safety.

¹²Haughtiness goes before destruction; humility precedes honor.

¹³What a shame, what folly, to give advice before listening to the facts!

¹⁴The human spirit can endure a sick body, but who can bear it if the spirit is crushed?

¹⁵Intelligent people are always open to new ideas. In fact, they look for them.

¹⁶Giving a gift works wonders; it may bring you before important people!

¹⁷Any story sounds true until someone sets the record straight.

¹⁸Casting lots can end arguments and settle disputes between powerful opponents.

¹⁹It's harder to make amends with an offended friend than to capture a fortified city. Arguments separate friends like a gate locked with iron bars.

²⁰Words satisfy the soul as food satisfies the stomach; the right words on a person's lips bring satisfaction.

²¹Those who love to talk will experience the consequences, for the tongue can kill or nourish life.

²²The man who finds a wife finds a treasure and receives favor from the LORD.

²³The poor plead for mercy; the rich answer with insults.

²⁴There are "friends" who destroy each other, but a real friend sticks closer than a brother.

Notes

_____

_____

_____

_____

_____

_____

_____

_____

_____

_____

_____

Notes

_____

_____

_____

_____

_____

_____

_____

_____

_____

_____

_____

_____

_____

_____

_____

_____

_____

_____

Psalm 91

1 Those who live in the shelter of the Most High
    will find rest in the shadow of the Almighty.
2 This I declare of the LORD:
    He alone is my refuge, my place of safety;
    He is my God, and I am trusting Him.
3 For He will rescue you from every trap
    and protect you from the fatal plague.
4 He will shield you with His wings.
    He will shelter you with His feathers.
    His faithful promises are your armor and
        protection.
5 Do not be afraid of the terrors of the night,
    nor fear the dangers of the day,
6 nor dread the plague that stalks in darkness,
    nor the disaster that strikes at midday.
7 Though a thousand fall at your side,
    though ten thousand are dying around you,
    these evils will not touch you.
8 But you will see it with your eyes;
    you will see how the wicked are punished.

⁹ If you make the LORD your refuge,
  if you make the Most High your shelter,
¹⁰ no evil will conquer you;
  no plague will come near your dwelling.
¹¹ For He orders His angels
  to protect you wherever you go.
¹² They will hold you with their hands
  to keep you from striking your foot on a stone.
¹³ You will trample down lions and poisonous
    snakes;
  you will crush fierce lions and serpents under your
    feet!

¹⁴ The LORD says, "I will rescue those who love Me.
  I will protect those who trust in My name.
¹⁵ When they call on Me, I will answer;
  I will be with them in trouble.
  I will rescue them and honor them.
¹⁶ I will satisfy them with a long life
  and give them My salvation."

Psalm 92

A psalm to be sung on the LORD's Day. A song.

¹ It is good to give thanks to the LORD, ✘
  to sing praises to the Most High. ✘

² It is good to proclaim Your unfailing love in the
      morning,
      Your faithfulness in the evening,
³ accompanied by the harp and lute
      and the harmony of the lyre.
⁴ You thrill me, LORD, with all You have done for me!
      I sing for joy because of what You have done.

⁵ O LORD, what great miracles You do!
      And how deep are Your thoughts.
⁶ Only an ignorant person would not know this!
      Only a fool would not understand it.
⁷ Although the wicked flourish like weeds,
      and evildoers blossom with success,
      there is only eternal destruction ahead of them.
⁸ But You are exalted in the heavens.
      You, O LORD, continue forever.
⁹ Your enemies, LORD, will surely perish;
      all evildoers will be scattered.

¹⁰ But You have made me as strong as a wild bull.
      How refreshed I am by Your power!
¹¹ With my own eyes I have seen the downfall of my
      enemies;
      with my own ears I have heard the defeat of my
      wicked opponents.
¹² But the godly will flourish like palm trees
      and grow strong like the cedars of Lebanon.

13 For they are transplanted into the LORD's own house.
> They flourish in the courts of our God.
14 Even in old age they will still produce fruit;
> they will remain vital and green.
15 They will declare, "The LORD is just!
> He is my rock!
> There is nothing but goodness in Him!"

Psalm 93

1 The LORD is king! He is robed in majesty.
> Indeed, the LORD is robed in majesty and armed with
>   strength.
 The world is firmly established;
> it cannot be shaken.

2 Your throne, O LORD, has been established from time
>   immemorial.
> You Yourself are from the everlasting past.
3 The mighty oceans have roared, O LORD.
> The mighty oceans roar like thunder;
> the mighty oceans roar as they pound the shore.
4 But mightier than the violent raging of the seas,
> mightier than the breakers on the shore—
> the LORD above is mightier than these!
5 Your royal decrees cannot be changed.
> The nature of Your reign, O LORD, is holiness forever.

Psalm 94

¹ O Lord, the God to whom vengeance belongs,
    O God of vengeance, let Your glorious justice
      be seen!
² Arise, O judge of the earth.
    Sentence the proud to the penalties they deserve.
³ How long, O Lord?
    How long will the wicked be allowed to gloat?
⁴ Hear their arrogance!
    How these evildoers boast!
⁵ They oppress Your people, Lord,
    hurting those You love.
⁶ They kill widows and foreigners
    and murder orphans.
⁷ "The Lord isn't looking," they say,
    "and besides, the God of Israel doesn't care."

⁸ Think again, you fools!
    When will you finally catch on?
⁹ Is the One who made your ears deaf?
    Is the One who formed your eyes blind?
¹⁰ He punishes the nations—won't He also punish you?
    He knows everything—doesn't He also know what
      you are doing?
¹¹ The Lord knows people's thoughts,
    that they are worthless!

¹² Happy are those whom You discipline, LORD,
    and those whom You teach from Your law.
¹³ You give them relief from troubled times
    until a pit is dug for the wicked.
¹⁴ The LORD will not reject His people;
    He will not abandon His own special possession.
¹⁵ Judgment will come again for the righteous,
    and those who are upright will have a reward.

¹⁶ Who will protect me from the wicked?
    Who will stand up for me against evildoers?
¹⁷ Unless the LORD had helped me,
    I would soon have died.
¹⁸ I cried out, "I'm slipping!"
    and Your unfailing love, O LORD, supported me.
¹⁹ When doubts filled my mind,
    Your comfort gave me renewed hope and cheer.

²⁰ Can unjust leaders claim that God is on their side—
    leaders who permit injustice by their laws?
²¹ They attack the righteous
    and condemn the innocent to death.
²² But the LORD is my fortress;
    my God is a mighty rock where I can hide.
²³ God will make the sins of evil people fall back upon
        them.
    He will destroy them for their sins.
    The LORD our God will destroy them.

Psalm 95

¹ Come, let us sing to the LORD!
   Let us give a joyous shout to the rock of our salvation!
² Let us come before Him with thanksgiving.
   Let us sing Him psalms of praise.
³ For the LORD is a great God,
   the great King above all gods.
⁴ He owns the depths of the earth,
   and even the mightiest mountains are His.
⁵ The sea belongs to Him, for He made it.
   His hands formed the dry land, too.

⁶ Come, let us worship and bow down.
   Let us kneel before the LORD our maker,
⁷   for He is our God.
 We are the people He watches over,
   the sheep under His care.

 Oh, that you would listen to His voice today!
⁸ The LORD says, "Don't harden your hearts as Israel did
      at Meribah,
   as they did at Massah in the wilderness.
⁹ For there your ancestors tried My patience;
   they courted My wrath though they had seen My many
      miracles.
¹⁰ For forty years I was angry with them, and I said,
   'They are a people whose hearts turn away from Me.

They refuse to do what I tell them.'
[11] So in My anger I made a vow:
'They will never enter My place of rest.'"

Proverbs 19

It is better to be poor and honest than to be a fool and dishonest.

[2] Zeal without knowledge is not good; a person who moves too quickly may go the wrong way.

[3] People ruin their lives by their own foolishness and then are angry at the LORD.

[4] Wealth makes many "friends"; poverty drives them away.

[5] A false witness will not go unpunished, nor will a liar escape.

[6] Many beg favors from a prince; everyone is the friend of a person who gives gifts!

[7] If the relatives of the poor despise them, how much more will their friends avoid them. The poor call after them, but they are gone.

[8] To acquire wisdom is to love oneself; people who cherish understanding will prosper.

[9] A false witness will not go unpunished, and a liar will be destroyed.

¹⁰It isn't right for a fool to live in luxury or for a slave to rule over princes!

¹¹People with good sense restrain their anger; they earn esteem by overlooking wrongs.

¹²The king's anger is like a lion's roar, but His favor is like dew on the grass.

¹³A foolish child is a calamity to a father; a nagging wife annoys like a constant dripping.

¹⁴Parents can provide their sons with an inheritance of houses and wealth, but only the LORD can give an understanding wife.

¹⁵A lazy person sleeps soundly—and goes hungry.

¹⁶Keep the commandments and keep your life; despising them leads to death.

¹⁷If you help the poor, you are lending to the LORD—and He will repay you!

¹⁸Discipline your children while there is hope. If you don't, you will ruin their lives.

¹⁹Short-tempered people must pay their own penalty. If you rescue them once, you will have to do it again.

²⁰Get all the advice and instruction you can, and be wise the rest of your life.

²¹You can make many plans, but the LORD's purpose will prevail.

²²Loyalty makes a person attractive. And it is better to be poor than dishonest.

²³Fear of the LORD gives life, security, and protection from harm.

²⁴Some people are so lazy that they won't even lift a finger to feed themselves.

²⁵If you punish a mocker, the simpleminded will learn a lesson; if you reprove the wise, they will be all the wiser.

²⁶Children who mistreat their father or chase away their mother are a public disgrace and an embarrassment.

²⁷If you stop listening to instruction, my child, you have turned your back on knowledge.

²⁸A corrupt witness makes a mockery of justice; the mouth of the wicked gulps down evil.

²⁹Mockers will be punished, and the backs of fools will be beaten.

Notes

_____

_____

_____

_____

_____

_____

_____

_____

_____

_____

_____

_____

_____

_____

_____

_____

_____

Psalm 96

¹ Sing a new song to the LORD!
  Let the whole earth sing to the LORD!
² Sing to the LORD; bless His name.
  Each day proclaim the good news that
    He saves.
³ Publish His glorious deeds among the nations.
  Tell everyone about the amazing things
    He does.
⁴ Great is the LORD! He is most worthy of praise!
  He is to be revered above all the gods.
⁵ The gods of other nations are merely idols,
  but the LORD made the heavens!
⁶ Honor and majesty surround Him;
  strength and beauty are in His sanctuary.

⁷ O nations of the world, recognize the LORD;
  recognize that the LORD is glorious and strong.
⁸ Give to the LORD the glory He deserves!
  Bring your offering and come to worship Him.
⁹ Worship the LORD in all His holy splendor.
  Let all the earth tremble before Him.

¹⁰ Tell all the nations that the LORD is king.
    The world is firmly established and cannot be shaken.
    He will judge all peoples fairly.
¹¹ Let the heavens be glad, and let the earth rejoice!
    Let the sea and everything in it shout His praise!
¹²   Let the fields and their crops burst forth with joy!
    Let the trees of the forest rustle with praise
¹³   before the LORD!
  For the LORD is coming!
    He is coming to judge the earth.
  He will judge the world with righteousness
    and all the nations with His truth.

Psalm 97

¹ The LORD is king! Let the earth rejoice!
    Let the farthest islands be glad.
² Clouds and darkness surround Him.
    Righteousness and justice are the foundation of His
        throne.
³ Fire goes forth before Him
    and burns up all His foes.
⁴ His lightning flashes out across the world.
    The earth sees and trembles.
⁵ The mountains melt like wax before the LORD,
    before the Lord of all the earth.

⁶ The heavens declare His righteousness;
   every nation sees His glory.
⁷ Those who worship idols are disgraced—
   all who brag about their worthless gods—
   for every god must bow to Him.
⁸ Jerusalem has heard and rejoiced,
   and all the cities of Judah are glad
   because of Your justice, LORD!
⁹ For You, O LORD, are most high over all the earth;
   You are exalted far above all gods.

¹⁰ You who love the LORD, hate evil!
   He protects the lives of His godly people
   and rescues them from the power of the wicked.
¹¹ Light shines on the godly,
   and joy on those who do right.
¹² May all who are godly be happy in the LORD
   and praise His holy name!

Psalm 98

A psalm.

¹ Sing a new song to the LORD,
   for He has done wonderful deeds.
   He has won a mighty victory
   by His power and holiness.

² The LORD has announced His victory
    and has revealed His righteousness to
      every nation!
³ He has remembered His promise to love and
      be faithful to Israel.
    The whole earth has seen the salvation of
      our God.

⁴ Shout to the LORD, all the earth;
    break out in praise and sing for joy!
⁵ Sing your praise to the LORD with the harp,
    with the harp and melodious song,
⁶   with trumpets and the sound of the
      ram's horn.
  Make a joyful symphony before the LORD,
      the King!

⁷ Let the sea and everything in it shout
      His praise!
    Let the earth and all living things
      join in.
⁸   Let the rivers clap their hands in glee!
    Let the hills sing out their songs of joy
⁹   before the LORD.
  For the LORD is coming to judge
      the earth.
    He will judge the world with justice,
    and the nations with fairness.

Psalm 99

¹ The LORD is king!
  Let the nations tremble!
 He sits on His throne between the
    cherubim.
  Let the whole earth quake!
² The LORD sits in majesty in Jerusalem,
    supreme above all the nations.
³ Let them praise Your great and awesome
    name.
  Your name is holy!
⁴ Mighty king, lover of justice,
  You have established fairness.
 You have acted with justice
    and righteousness throughout Israel.
⁵ Exalt the LORD our God!
  Bow low before His feet, for He
    is holy!

⁶ Moses and Aaron were among His priests;
    Samuel also called on His name.
 They cried to the LORD for help,
    and He answered them.
⁷ He spoke to them from the pillar of cloud,
    and they followed the decrees and principles
      He gave them.

⁸ O LORD our God, You answered them.
　　You were a forgiving God,
　　but You punished them when they went wrong.

⁹ Exalt the LORD our God
　　and worship at His holy mountain in Jerusalem,
　　for the LORD our God is holy!

Psalm 100

A psalm of thanksgiving.

¹ Shout with joy to the LORD, O earth!
²　Worship the LORD with gladness.
　　Come before Him, singing with joy.
³ Acknowledge that the LORD is God!
　　He made us, and we are His.
　　We are His people, the sheep of
　　　His pasture.

⁴ Enter His gates with thanksgiving;
　　go into His courts with praise.
　　Give thanks to Him and bless His name.
⁵ For the LORD is good.
　　His unfailing love continues forever,
　　and His faithfulness continues to each
　　　generation.

Proverbs 20

Wine produces mockers; liquor leads to brawls. Whoever is led astray by drink cannot be wise.

²The king's fury is like a lion's roar; to rouse his anger is to risk your life.

³Avoiding a fight is a mark of honor; only fools insist on quarreling.

⁴If you are too lazy to plow in the right season, you will have no food at the harvest.

⁵Though good advice lies deep within a person's heart, the wise will draw it out.

⁶Many will say they are loyal friends, but who can find one who is really faithful?

⁷The godly walk with integrity; blessed are their children after them.

⁸When a king judges, he carefully weighs all the evidence, distinguishing the bad from the good.

⁹Who can say, "I have cleansed my heart; I am pure and free from sin"?

¹⁰The LORD despises double standards of every kind.

¹¹Even children are known by the way they act, whether their conduct is pure and right.

¹²Ears to hear and eyes to see—both are gifts from the LORD.

¹³If you love sleep, you will end in poverty. Keep your eyes open, and there will be plenty to eat!

¹⁴The buyer haggles over the price, saying, "It's worthless," then brags about getting a bargain!

¹⁵Wise speech is rarer and more valuable than gold and rubies.

¹⁶Be sure to get collateral from anyone who guarantees the debt of a stranger. Get a deposit if someone guarantees the debt of a foreigner.

¹⁷Stolen bread tastes sweet, but it turns to gravel in the mouth.

¹⁸Plans succeed through good counsel; don't go to war without the advice of others.

¹⁹A gossip tells secrets, so don't hang around with someone who talks too much.

²⁰If you curse your father or mother, the lamp of your life will be snuffed out.

²¹An inheritance obtained early in life is not a blessing in the end.

²²Don't say, "I will get even for this wrong." Wait for the LORD to handle the matter.

²³The LORD despises double standards; He is not pleased by dishonest scales.

²⁴How can we understand the road we travel? It is the LORD who directs our steps.

²⁵It is dangerous to make a rash promise to God before counting the cost.

²⁶A wise king finds the wicked, lays them out like wheat, then runs the crushing wheel over them.

[27]The LORD's searchlight penetrates the human spirit exposing every hidden motive.

[28]Unfailing love and faithfulness protect the king; his throne is made secure through love.

[29]The glory of the young is their strength; the gray hair of experience is the splendor of the old.

[30]Physical punishment cleanses away evil; such discipline purifies the heart.

Notes

_____

_____

_____

_____

_____

_____

_____

_____

_____

_____

_____

Psalm 101

A psalm of David.

¹ I will sing of Your love and justice.
　 I will praise You, LORD, with songs.
² I will be careful to live a blameless life—
　 when will You come to my aid?
　I will lead a life of integrity
　 in my own home.
³ I will refuse to look at
　 anything vile and vulgar.
　I hate all crooked dealings;
　 I will have nothing to do with them.
⁴ I will reject perverse ideas
　 and stay away from every evil.
⁵ I will not tolerate people who slander their
　　 neighbors.
　 I will not endure conceit and pride.

⁶ I will keep a protective eye on the godly,
　 so they may dwell with me in safety.
　Only those who are above reproach
　 will be allowed to serve me.

⁷ I will not allow deceivers to serve me,
  and liars will not be allowed to enter my
    presence.
⁸ My daily task will be to ferret out criminals
  and free the city of the LORD from their grip.

Psalm 102

A prayer of one overwhelmed with trouble, pouring out problems before the LORD.

¹ LORD, hear my prayer!
    Listen to my plea!
² Don't turn away from me
    in my time of distress.
  Bend down Your ear
    and answer me quickly when I call to You,
³   for my days disappear like smoke,
    and my bones burn like red-hot coals.
⁴ My heart is sick, withered like grass,
    and I have lost my appetite.
⁵ Because of my groaning,
    I am reduced to skin and bones.
⁶ I am like an owl in the desert,
    like a lonely owl in a far-off wilderness.
⁷ I lie awake,
    lonely as a solitary bird on the roof.

⁸ My enemies taunt me day after day.

    They mock and curse me.

⁹ I eat ashes instead of my food.

    My tears run down into my drink

¹⁰ because of Your anger and wrath.

    For You have picked me up and thrown me out.

¹¹ My life passes as swiftly as the evening shadows.

    I am withering like grass.

¹² But You, O LORD, will rule forever.

    Your fame will endure to every generation.

¹³ You will arise and have mercy on Jerusalem—

    and now is the time to pity her,

    now is the time You promised to help.

¹⁴ For Your people love every stone in her walls

    and show favor even to the dust in her streets.

¹⁵ And the nations will tremble before the LORD.

    The kings of the earth will tremble before His glory.

¹⁶ For the LORD will rebuild Jerusalem.

    He will appear in His glory.

¹⁷ He will listen to the prayers of the destitute.

    He will not reject their pleas.

¹⁸ Let this be recorded for future generations,

    so that a nation yet to be created will praise the LORD.

¹⁹ Tell them the LORD looked down

    from His heavenly sanctuary.

He looked to the earth from heaven

20   to hear the groans of the prisoners,
       to release those condemned to die.
21 And so the LORD's fame will be celebrated
          in Zion,
       His praises in Jerusalem,
22 when multitudes gather together
       and kingdoms come to worship the LORD.

23 He has cut me down in midlife,
       shortening my days.
24 But I cried to Him, "My God, who lives
          forever,
       don't take my life while I am still so
          young!
25 In ages past You laid the foundation of
          the earth,
       and the heavens are the work of Your hands.
26 Even they will perish, but You remain forever;
       they will wear out like old clothing.
    You will change them like a garment,
       and they will fade away.
27 But You are always the same;
       Your years never end.
28 The children of Your people
       will live in security.
    Their children's children
       will thrive in Your presence."

Psalm 103

A psalm of David.

¹ Praise the LORD, I tell myself;
   with my whole heart, I will praise His holy name.
² Praise the LORD, I tell myself,
   and never forget the good things He does for me.
³ He forgives all my sins
   and heals all my diseases.
⁴ He ransoms me from death
   and surrounds me with love and tender mercies.
⁵ He fills my life with good things.
   My youth is renewed like the eagle's!
⁶ The LORD gives righteousness
   and justice to all who are treated unfairly.
⁷ He revealed His character to Moses
   and His deeds to the people of Israel.
⁸ The LORD is merciful and gracious;
   He is slow to get angry and full of unfailing love.
⁹ He will not constantly accuse us,
   nor remain angry forever.
¹⁰ He has not punished us for all our sins,
   nor does He deal with us as we deserve.
¹¹ For His unfailing love toward those who fear Him
   is as great as the height of the heavens above the earth.
¹² He has removed our rebellious acts
   as far away from us as the east is from the west.

¹³ The L<small>ORD</small> is like a father to His children,
    tender and compassionate to those
        who fear Him.
¹⁴ For He understands how weak we are;
    He knows we are only dust.
¹⁵ Our days on earth are like grass;
    like wildflowers, we bloom and die.
¹⁶ The wind blows, and we are gone—
    as though we had never been here.
¹⁷ But the love of the L<small>ORD</small> remains forever
    with those who fear Him.
  His salvation extends to the children's
        children
¹⁸   of those who are faithful to His covenant,
    of those who obey His commandments!

¹⁹ The L<small>ORD</small> has made the heavens His throne;
    from there He rules over everything.
²⁰ Praise the L<small>ORD</small>, you angels of His,
    you mighty creatures who carry out
        His plans,
    listening for each of His commands.
²¹ Yes, praise the L<small>ORD</small>, you armies of angels
    who serve Him and do His will!
²² Praise the L<small>ORD</small>, everything He has created,
    everywhere in His kingdom.
    As for me—I, too, will praise the L<small>ORD</small>.

Proverbs 21

The king's heart is like a stream of water directed by the LORD; He turns it wherever He pleases.

²People may think they are doing what is right, but the LORD examines the heart.

³The LORD is more pleased when we do what is just and right than when we give Him sacrifices.

⁴Haughty eyes, a proud heart, and evil actions are all sin.

⁵Good planning and hard work lead to prosperity, but hasty shortcuts lead to poverty.

⁶Wealth created by lying is a vanishing mist and a deadly trap.

⁷Because the wicked refuse to do what is just, their violence boomerangs and destroys them.

⁸The guilty walk a crooked path; the innocent travel a straight road.

⁹It is better to live alone in the corner of an attic than with a contentious wife in a lovely home.

¹⁰Evil people love to harm others; their neighbors get no mercy from them.

¹¹A simpleton can learn only by seeing mockers punished; a wise person learns from instruction.

¹²The Righteous One knows what is going on in the homes of the wicked; He will bring the wicked to disaster.

¹³Those who shut their ears to the cries of the poor will be ignored in their own time of need.

¹⁴A secret gift calms anger; a secret bribe pacifies fury.

¹⁵Justice is a joy to the godly, but it causes dismay among evildoers.

¹⁶The person who strays from common sense will end up in the company of the dead.

¹⁷Those who love pleasure become poor; wine and luxury are not the way to riches.

¹⁸Sometimes the wicked are punished to save the godly, and the treacherous for the upright.

¹⁹It is better to live alone in the desert than with a crabby, complaining wife.

²⁰The wise have wealth and luxury, but fools spend whatever they get.

²¹Whoever pursues godliness and unfailing love will find life, godliness, and honor.

²²The wise conquer the city of the strong and level the fortress in which they trust.

²³If you keep your mouth shut, you will stay out of trouble.

²⁴Mockers are proud and haughty; they act with boundless arrogance.

²⁵The desires of lazy people will be their ruin, for their hands refuse to work. ²⁶They are always greedy for more, while the godly love to give!

²⁷God loathes the sacrifice of an evil person, especially when it is brought with ulterior motives.

²⁸A false witness will be cut off, but an attentive witness will be allowed to speak.

²⁹The wicked put up a bold front, but the upright proceed with care.

³⁰Human plans, no matter how wise or well advised, cannot stand against the LORD.

³¹The horses are prepared for battle, but the victory belongs to the LORD.

Notes

_____

_____

_____

_____

_____

_____

_____

_____

_____

_____

_____

Psalm 104

¹ Praise the LORD, I tell myself;
    O LORD my God, how great You are!
  You are robed with honor and with majesty;
²   You are dressed in a robe of light.
  You stretch out the starry curtain of the heavens;
³   You lay out the rafters of Your home in the rain clouds.
  You make the clouds Your chariots;
    You ride upon the wings of the wind.
⁴ The winds are Your messengers;
    flames of fire are Your servants.

⁵ You placed the world on its foundation
    so it would never be moved.
⁶ You clothed the earth with floods of water,
    water that covered even the mountains.
⁷ At the sound of Your rebuke, the water fled;
    at the sound of Your thunder, it fled away.
⁸ Mountains rose and valleys sank
    to the levels You decreed.
⁹ Then You set a firm boundary for the seas,
    so they would never again cover the earth.

¹⁰ You make the springs pour water into ravines,
 so streams gush down from the mountains.
¹¹ They provide water for all the animals,
 and the wild donkeys quench their thirst.
¹² The birds nest beside the streams
 and sing among the branches of the trees.
¹³ You send rain on the mountains from Your heavenly
  home,
 and You fill the earth with the fruit of Your labor.
¹⁴ You cause grass to grow for the cattle.
 You cause plants to grow for people to use.
 You allow them to produce food from the earth—
¹⁵ wine to make them glad,
 olive oil as lotion for their skin,
 and bread to give them strength.
¹⁶ The trees of the LORD are well cared for—
 the cedars of Lebanon that He planted.
¹⁷ There the birds make their nests,
 and the storks make their homes in the firs.
¹⁸ High in the mountains are pastures for the wild goats,
 and the rocks form a refuge for rock badgers.
¹⁹ You made the moon to mark the seasons
 and the sun that knows when to set.
²⁰ You send the darkness, and it becomes night,
 when all the forest animals prowl about.
²¹ Then the young lions roar for their food,
 but they are dependent on God.

²² At dawn they slink back
    into their dens to rest.
²³ Then people go off to their work;
    they labor until the evening shadows fall again.

²⁴ O LORD, what a variety of things You have made!
    In wisdom You have made them all.
    The earth is full of Your creatures.
²⁵ Here is the ocean, vast and wide,
    teeming with life of every kind,
    both great and small.
²⁶ See the ships sailing along,
    and Leviathan, which You made to play in the sea.
²⁷ Every one of these depends on You
    to give them their food as they need it.
²⁸ When You supply it, they gather it.
    You open Your hand to feed them, and they are
        satisfied.
²⁹ But if You turn away from them, they panic.
    When You take away their breath, they die
    and turn again to dust.
³⁰ When You send Your Spirit, new life is born
    to replenish all the living of the earth.

³¹ May the glory of the LORD last forever!
    The LORD rejoices in all He has made!
³² The earth trembles at His glance;
    the mountains burst into flame at His touch.

³³ I will sing to the LORD as long as I live.

 I will praise my God to my last breath!

³⁴ May He be pleased by all these thoughts about Him,

 for I rejoice in the LORD.

³⁵ Let all sinners vanish from the face of the earth;

 let the wicked disappear forever.

As for me—I will praise the LORD!

Praise the LORD!

Psalm 105

¹ Give thanks to the LORD and proclaim

 His greatness.

 Let the whole world know what He has done.

² Sing to Him; yes, sing His praises.

 Tell everyone about His miracles.

³ Exult in His holy name;

 O worshipers of the LORD, rejoice!

⁴ Search for the LORD and for His strength,

 and keep on searching.

⁵ Think of the wonderful works He has done,

 the miracles and the judgments He handed down,

⁶ O children of Abraham, God's servant,

 O descendants of Jacob, God's chosen one.

⁷ He is the LORD our God.

 His rule is seen throughout the land.

⁸ He always stands by His covenant—
    the commitment He made to a thousand generations.
⁹ This is the covenant He made with Abraham
    and the oath He swore to Isaac.
¹⁰ He confirmed it to Jacob as a decree,
    to the people of Israel as a never-ending treaty:
¹¹ "I will give You the land of Canaan
    as Your special possession."

¹² He said this when they were few in number,
    a tiny group of strangers in Canaan.
¹³ They wandered back and forth between nations,
    from one kingdom to another.
¹⁴ Yet He did not let anyone oppress them.
    He warned kings on their behalf:
¹⁵ "Do not touch these people I have chosen,
    and do not hurt my prophets."
¹⁶ He called for a famine on the land of Canaan,
    cutting off its food supply.
¹⁷ Then He sent someone to Egypt ahead of them—
    Joseph, who was sold as a slave.
¹⁸ There in prison, they bruised his feet with fetters
    and placed his neck in an iron collar.
¹⁹ Until the time came to fulfill his word,
    the LORD tested Joseph's character.
²⁰ Then Pharaoh sent for him and set him free;
    the ruler of the nation opened his prison door.

²¹ Joseph was put in charge of all the king's household;
    he became ruler over all the king's possessions.
²² He could instruct the king's aides as He pleased
    and teach the king's advisers.

²³ Then Israel arrived in Egypt;
    Jacob lived as a foreigner in the land of Ham.
²⁴ And the LORD multiplied the people of Israel
    until they became too mighty for their enemies.
²⁵ Then He turned the Egyptians against the Israelites,
    and they plotted against the LORD's servants.

²⁶ But the LORD sent Moses His servant,
    along with Aaron, whom He had chosen.
²⁷ They performed miraculous signs among the Egyptians,
    and miracles in the land of Ham.
²⁸ The LORD blanketed Egypt in darkness,
    for they had defied His commands to let His people go.
²⁹ He turned the nation's water into blood,
    poisoning all the fish.
³⁰ Then frogs overran the land;
    they were found even in the king's private rooms.
³¹ When He spoke, flies descended on the Egyptians,
    and gnats swarmed across Egypt.
³² Instead of rain, He sent murderous hail,
    and flashes of lightning overwhelmed the land.
³³ He ruined their grapevines and fig trees
    and shattered all the trees.

³⁴ He spoke, and hordes of locusts came—
    locusts beyond number.
³⁵ They ate up everything green in the land,
    destroying all the crops.
³⁶ Then He killed the oldest child in each Egyptian home,
    the pride and joy of each family.

³⁷ But He brought His people safely out of Egypt, loaded
        with silver and gold;
    there were no sick or feeble people among them.
³⁸ Egypt was glad when they were gone,
    for the dread of them was great.
³⁹ The LORD spread out a cloud above them as a covering
    and gave them a great fire to light the darkness.
⁴⁰ They asked for meat, and He sent them quail;
    He gave them manna—bread from heaven.
⁴¹ He opened up a rock, and water gushed out
    to form a river through the dry and barren land.
⁴² For He remembered His sacred promise
    to Abraham His servant.
⁴³ So He brought His people out of Egypt with joy,
    His chosen ones with rejoicing.
⁴⁴ He gave His people the lands of pagan nations,
    and they harvested crops that others had planted.
⁴⁵ All this happened so they would follow His principles
    and obey His laws.

Praise the LORD!

Proverbs 22

Choose a good reputation over great riches, for being held in high esteem is better than having silver or gold.

²The rich and the poor have this in common: The LORD made them both.

³A prudent person foresees the danger ahead and takes precautions; the simpleton goes blindly on and suffers the consequences.

⁴True humility and fear of the LORD lead to riches, honor, and long life.

⁵The deceitful walk a thorny, treacherous road; whoever values life will stay away.

⁶Teach your children to choose the right path, and when they are older, they will remain upon it.

⁷Just as the rich rule the poor, so the borrower is servant to the lender.

⁸Those who plant seeds of injustice will harvest disaster, and their reign of terror will end.

⁹Blessed are those who are generous, because they feed the poor.

¹⁰Throw out the mocker, and fighting, quarrels, and insults will disappear.

¹¹Anyone who loves a pure heart and gracious speech is the king's friend.

¹²The LORD preserves knowledge, but He ruins the plans of the deceitful.

¹³The lazy person is full of excuses, saying, "If I go outside, I might meet a lion in the street and be killed!"

¹⁴The mouth of an immoral woman is a deep pit; those living under the LORD's displeasure will fall into it.

¹⁵A youngster's heart is filled with foolishness, but discipline will drive it away.

¹⁶A person who gets ahead by oppressing the poor or by showering gifts on the rich will end in poverty.

¹⁷Listen to the words of the wise; apply your heart to my instruction. ¹⁸For it is good to keep these sayings deep within yourself, always ready on your lips. ¹⁹I am teaching you today—yes, you—so you will trust in the LORD. ²⁰I have written thirty sayings for you, filled with advice and knowledge. ²¹In this way, you may know the truth and bring an accurate report to those who sent you.

²²Do not rob the poor because they are poor or exploit the needy in court. ²³For the LORD is their defender. He will injure anyone who injures them.

²⁴Keep away from angry, short-tempered people, ²⁵or you will learn to be like them and endanger your soul.

²⁶Do not co-sign another person's note or put up a guarantee for someone else's loan. ²⁷If you can't pay it, even your bed will be snatched from under you.

²⁸Do not steal your neighbor's property by moving the ancient boundary markers set up by your ancestors.

²⁹Do you see any truly competent workers? They will serve kings rather than ordinary people.

Notes

_____

_____

_____

_____

_____

_____

_____

_____

_____

_____

_____

_____

_____

_____

_____

_____

_____

_____

_____

_____

Notes

_____

_____

_____

_____

_____

_____

_____

_____

_____

_____

_____

_____

_____

_____

_____

_____

_____

_____

_____

_____

Psalm 106

¹ Praise the LORD!

Give thanks to the LORD, for He is good!
His faithful love endures forever.
² Who can list the glorious miracles of the LORD?
Who can ever praise Him half enough?
³ Happy are those who deal justly with others
and always do what is right.

⁴ Remember me, too, LORD, when You show favor
to Your people;
come to me with Your salvation.
⁵ Let me share in the prosperity of Your chosen ones.
Let me rejoice in the joy of Your people;
let me praise You with those who are Your heritage.

⁶ Both we and our ancestors have sinned.
We have done wrong! We have acted wickedly!
⁷ Our ancestors in Egypt
were not impressed by the LORD's miracles.
They soon forgot His many acts of kindness to them.
Instead, they rebelled against Him at the Red Sea.

⁸ Even so, He saved them—
   to defend the honor of His name
   and to demonstrate His mighty power.
⁹ He commanded the Red Sea to divide, and a dry path
      appeared.
   He led Israel across the sea bottom that was as dry as a
      desert.
¹⁰ So He rescued them from their enemies
   and redeemed them from their foes.
¹¹ Then the water returned and covered their enemies;
   not one of them survived.
¹² Then at last His people believed His promises.
   Then they finally sang His praise.

¹³ Yet how quickly they forgot what He had done!
   They wouldn't wait for His counsel!
¹⁴ In the wilderness, their desires ran wild,
   testing God's patience in that dry land.
¹⁵ So He gave them what they asked for,
   but He sent a plague along with it.
¹⁶ The people in the camp were jealous of Moses
   and envious of Aaron, the LORD's holy priest.
¹⁷ Because of this, the earth opened up;
   it swallowed Dathan
   and buried Abiram and the other rebels.
¹⁸ Fire fell upon their followers;
   a flame consumed the wicked.

¹⁹ The people made a calf at Mount Sinai;
    they bowed before an image made of gold.
²⁰ They traded their glorious God
    for a statue of a grass-eating ox!
²¹ They forgot God, their savior,
    who had done such great things in Egypt—
²² such wonderful things in that land,
    such awesome deeds at the Red Sea.
²³ So He declared He would destroy them.
    But Moses, His chosen one, stepped between the LORD
        and the people.
    He begged Him to turn from His anger and not
        destroy them.

²⁴ The people refused to enter the pleasant land,
    for they wouldn't believe His promise to care for them.
²⁵ Instead, they grumbled in their tents
    and refused to obey the LORD.
²⁶ Therefore, He swore
    that He would kill them in the wilderness,
²⁷ that He would scatter their descendants among the
        nations,
    exiling them to distant lands.

²⁸ Then our ancestors joined in the worship of Baal at Peor;
    they even ate sacrifices offered to the dead!
²⁹ They angered the LORD with all these things,
    so a plague broke out among them.

³⁰ But Phinehas had the courage to step in,
    and the plague was stopped.
³¹ So He has been regarded as a righteous man
    ever since that time.

³² At Meribah, too, they angered the LORD,
    causing Moses serious trouble.
³³ They made Moses angry,
    and he spoke foolishly.

³⁴ Israel failed to destroy the nations in the land,
    as the LORD had told them to.
³⁵ Instead, they mingled among the pagans
    and adopted their evil customs.
³⁶ They worshiped their idols,
    and this led to their downfall.
³⁷ They even sacrificed their sons
    and their daughters to the demons.
³⁸ They shed innocent blood,
    the blood of their sons and daughters.
  By sacrificing them to the idols of Canaan,
    they polluted the land with murder.
³⁹ They defiled themselves by their evil deeds,
    and their love of idols was adultery in the
      LORD's sight.

⁴⁰ That is why the LORD's anger burned against His people,
    and He abhorred His own special possession.

⁴¹ He handed them over to pagan nations,
    and those who hated them ruled over them.
⁴² Their enemies crushed them
    and brought them under their cruel
       power.
⁴³ Again and again He delivered them,
    but they continued to rebel against Him,
    and they were finally destroyed by
       their sin.
⁴⁴ Even so, He pitied them in their distress
    and listened to their cries.
⁴⁵ He remembered His covenant with them
    and relented because of His unfailing
       love.
⁴⁶ He even caused their captors
    to treat them with kindness.

⁴⁷ O LORD our God, save us!
    Gather us back from among the
       nations,
so we can thank Your holy name
    and rejoice and praise You.

⁴⁸ Blessed be the LORD, the God of Israel,
    from everlasting to everlasting!
Let all the people say, "Amen!"

Praise the LORD!

Psalm 107

¹ Give thanks to the LORD, for He is good!
    His faithful love endures forever.
² Has the LORD redeemed you? Then speak out!
    Tell others He has saved you from your enemies.
³ For He has gathered the exiles from many lands,
    from east and west, from north and south.

⁴ Some wandered in the desert,
    lost and homeless.
⁵ Hungry and thirsty,
    they nearly died.
⁶ "LORD, help!" they cried in their trouble,
    and He rescued them from their distress.
⁷ He led them straight to safety,
    to a city where they could live.
⁸ Let them praise the LORD for His great love
    and for all His wonderful deeds to them.
⁹ For He satisfies the thirsty
    and fills the hungry with good things.

¹⁰ Some sat in darkness and deepest gloom,
    miserable prisoners in chains.
¹¹ They rebelled against the words of God,
    scorning the counsel of the Most High.
¹² That is why He broke them with hard labor;
    they fell, and no one helped them rise again.

¹³ "LORD, help!" they cried in their trouble,
    and He saved them from their distress.
¹⁴ He led them from the darkness and deepest gloom;
    He snapped their chains.
¹⁵ Let them praise the LORD for His great love
    and for all His wonderful deeds to them.
¹⁶ For He broke down their prison gates of bronze;
    He cut apart their bars of iron.

¹⁷ Some were fools in their rebellion;
    they suffered for their sins.
¹⁸ Their appetites were gone,
    and death was near.
¹⁹ "LORD, help!" they cried in their trouble,
    and He saved them from their distress.
²⁰ He spoke, and they were healed—
    snatched from the door of death.
²¹ Let them praise the LORD for His great love
    and for all His wonderful deeds to them.
²² Let them offer sacrifices of thanksgiving
    and sing joyfully about His glorious acts.

²³ Some went off in ships,
    plying the trade routes of the world.
²⁴ They, too, observed the LORD's power in action,
    His impressive works on the deepest seas.
²⁵ He spoke, and the winds rose,
    stirring up the waves.

²⁶ Their ships were tossed to the heavens
    and sank again to the depths;
    the sailors cringed in terror.
²⁷ They reeled and staggered like drunkards
    and were at their wits' end.
²⁸ "LORD, help!" they cried in their trouble,
    and He saved them from their distress.
²⁹ He calmed the storm to a whisper
    and stilled the waves.
³⁰ What a blessing was that stillness
    as He brought them safely into harbor!
³¹ Let them praise the LORD for His great love
    and for all His wonderful deeds to them.
³² Let them exalt Him publicly before the congregation
    and before the leaders of the nation.

³³ He changes rivers into deserts,
    and springs of water into dry land.
³⁴ He turns the fruitful land into salty wastelands,
    because of the wickedness of those who live there.
³⁵ But He also turns deserts into pools of water,
    the dry land into flowing springs.
³⁶ He brings the hungry to settle there
    and build their cities.
³⁷ They sow their fields, plant their vineyards,
    and harvest their bumper crops.
³⁸ How He blesses them!

They raise large families there,
and their herds of cattle increase.

³⁹ When they decrease in number and become
impoverished
through oppression, trouble, and sorrow,
⁴⁰ the LORD pours contempt on their princes,
causing them to wander in trackless wastelands.
⁴¹ But He rescues the poor from their distress
and increases their families like vast flocks
of sheep.
⁴² The godly will see these things and be glad,
while the wicked are stricken silent.
⁴³ Those who are wise will take all this to heart;
they will see in our history the faithful love of
the LORD.

Proverbs 23

When dining with a ruler, pay attention to what is put
before you. ²If you are a big eater, put a knife to your
throat, ³and don't desire all the delicacies—deception may
be involved.

⁴Don't weary yourself trying to get rich. Why waste your
time? ⁵For riches can disappear as though they had the
wings of a bird!

⁶Don't eat with people who are stingy; don't desire their delicacies. ⁷"Eat and drink," they say, but they don't mean it. They are always thinking about how much it costs. ⁸You will vomit up the delicious food they serve, and you will have to take back your words of appreciation for their "kindness."

⁹Don't waste your breath on fools, for they will despise the wisest advice.

¹⁰Don't steal the land of defenseless orphans by moving the ancient boundary markers, ¹¹for their Redeemer is strong. He Himself will bring their charges against you.

¹²Commit yourself to instruction; attune your ears to hear words of knowledge.

¹³Don't fail to correct your children. They won't die if you spank them. ¹⁴Physical discipline may well save them from death.

¹⁵My child, how I will rejoice if you become wise. ¹⁶Yes, my heart will thrill when you speak what is right and just.

¹⁷Don't envy sinners, but always continue to fear the LORD. ¹⁸For surely you have a future ahead of you; your hope will not be disappointed.

¹⁹My child, listen and be wise. Keep your heart on the right course. ²⁰Do not carouse with drunkards and gluttons, ²¹for they are on their way to poverty. Too much sleep clothes a person with rags.

²²Listen to your father, who gave you life, and don't despise your mother's experience when she is old. ²³Get the

truth and don't ever sell it; also get wisdom, discipline, and discernment. ²⁴The father of godly children has cause for joy. What a pleasure it is to have wise children. ²⁵So give your parents joy! May she who gave you birth be happy.

²⁶O my son, give me your heart. May your eyes delight in my ways of wisdom. ²⁷A prostitute is a deep pit; an adulterous woman is treacherous. ²⁸She hides and waits like a robber, looking for another victim who will be unfaithful to his wife.

²⁹Who has anguish? Who has sorrow? Who is always fighting? Who is always complaining? Who has unnecessary bruises? Who has bloodshot eyes? ³⁰It is the one who spends long hours in the taverns, trying out new drinks. ³¹Don't let the sparkle and smooth taste of wine deceive you. ³²For in the end it bites like a poisonous serpent; it stings like a viper. ³³You will see hallucinations, and you will say crazy things. ³⁴You will stagger like a sailor tossed at sea, clinging to a swaying mast. ³⁵And you will say, "They hit me, but I didn't feel it. I didn't even know it when they beat me up. When will I wake up so I can have another drink?"

Notes

_____

_____

_____

_____

_____

_____

_____

_____

_____

_____

_____

_____

_____

_____

_____

_____

_____

_____

_____

Psalm 108

A psalm of David. A song.

¹ My heart is confident in You, O God;
no wonder I can sing Your praises!
Wake up, my soul!
² Wake up, O harp and lyre!
I will waken the dawn with my song.
³ I will thank You, LORD, in front of all the people.
I will sing Your praises among the nations.
⁴ For Your unfailing love is higher than the heavens.
Your faithfulness reaches to the clouds.
⁵ Be exalted, O God, above the highest heavens.
May Your glory shine over all the earth.

⁶ Use Your strong right arm to save me,
and rescue Your beloved people.
⁷ God has promised this by His holiness:
"I will divide up Shechem with joy.
I will measure out the valley of Succoth.
⁸ Gilead is Mine,
and Manasseh is Mine.
Ephraim will produce My warriors,
and Judah will produce My kings.

⁹ Moab will become My lowly servant,
    and Edom will be My slave.
    I will shout in triumph over the Philistines."

¹⁰ But who will bring me into the fortified city?
    Who will bring me victory over Edom?
¹¹ Have You rejected us, O God?
    Will You no longer march with our armies?
¹² Oh, please help us against our enemies,
    for all human help is useless.
¹³ With God's help we will do mighty things,
    for He will trample down our foes.

Psalm 109

For the choir director: A psalm of David.

¹ O God, whom I praise,
    don't stand silent and aloof
² while the wicked slander me
    and tell lies about me.
³ They are all around me with their hateful words,
    and they fight against me for no reason.
⁴ I love them, but they try to destroy me—
    even as I am praying for them!
⁵ They return evil for good,
    and hatred for my love.

⁶ Arrange for an evil person to turn on him.
   Send an accuser to bring him to trial.
⁷ When his case is called for judgment,
   let him be pronounced guilty.
   Count his prayers as sins.
⁸ Let his years be few;
   let his position be given to someone else.
⁹ May his children become fatherless,
   and may his wife become a widow.
¹⁰ May his children wander as beggars;
   may they be evicted from their ruined homes.
¹¹ May creditors seize his entire estate,
   and strangers take all he has earned.
¹² Let no one be kind to him;
   let no one pity his fatherless children.
¹³ May all his offspring die.
   May his family name be blotted out in a single
      generation.
¹⁴ May the LORD never forget the sins of his ancestors;
   may his mother's sins never be erased from the record.
¹⁵ May these sins always remain before the LORD,
   but may his name be cut off from human memory.
¹⁶ For he refused all kindness to others;
   he persecuted the poor and needy,
   and he hounded the brokenhearted to death.
¹⁷ He loved to curse others;
   now You curse him.

He never blessed others;
　　now don't You bless him.
¹⁸ Cursing is as much a part of him as his clothing,
　　or as the water he drinks,
　　or the rich food he eats.
¹⁹ Now may his curses return and cling to him like
　　clothing;
　　may they be tied around him like a belt.

²⁰ May those curses become the LORD's punishment for my
　　accusers
　　who are plotting against my life.
²¹ But deal well with me, O Sovereign LORD,
　　for the sake of Your own reputation!
Rescue me because You are so faithful and good.
²²　For I am poor and needy,
　　and my heart is full of pain.
²³ I am fading like a shadow at dusk;
　　I am falling like a grasshopper that is brushed aside.
²⁴ My knees are weak from fasting,
　　and I am skin and bones.
²⁵ I am an object of mockery to people everywhere;
　　when they see me, they shake their heads.

²⁶ Help me, O LORD my God!
　　Save me because of Your unfailing love.
²⁷ Let them see that this is Your doing,
　　that You Yourself have done it, LORD.

²⁸ Then let them curse me if they like,
    but You will bless me!
  When they attack me, they will be disgraced!
    But I, Your servant, will go right on rejoicing!
²⁹ Make their humiliation obvious to all;
    clothe my accusers with disgrace.
³⁰ But I will give repeated thanks to the LORD,
    praising Him to everyone.
³¹ For He stands beside the needy,
    ready to save them from those who condemn them.

Psalm 110

A psalm of David.

¹ The LORD said to my Lord,
    "Sit in honor at My right hand
  until I humble Your enemies,
    making them a footstool under Your feet."

² The LORD will extend Your powerful dominion from
      Jerusalem;
    You will rule over Your enemies.
³ In that day of battle,
    Your people will serve You willingly.
  Arrayed in holy garments,
    Your vigor will be renewed each day like the morning
      dew.

⁴ The LORD has taken an oath and will not break His vow:
   "You are a priest forever in the line of Melchizedek."
⁵ The Lord stands at Your right hand to protect You.
   He will strike down many kings in the day of His
      anger.
⁶ He will punish the nations
   and fill them with their dead;
 He will shatter heads
   over the whole earth.
⁷ But He Himself will be refreshed from brooks along the
      way.
   He will be victorious.

Psalm 111

¹ Praise the LORD!

 I will thank the LORD with all my heart
   as I meet with His godly people.
² How amazing are the deeds of the LORD!
   All who delight in Him should ponder them.
³ Everything He does reveals His glory and majesty.
   His righteousness never fails.
⁴ Who can forget the wonders He performs?
   How gracious and merciful is our LORD!
⁵ He gives food to those who trust Him;

He always remembers His covenant.
⁶ He has shown His great power to His people
    by giving them the lands of other nations.
⁷ All He does is just and good,
    and all His commandments are trustworthy.
⁸ They are forever true,
    to be obeyed faithfully and with integrity.
⁹ He has paid a full ransom for His people.
    He has guaranteed His covenant with them forever.
    What a holy, awe-inspiring name He has!
¹⁰ Reverence for the LORD is the foundation of true
    wisdom.
    The rewards of wisdom come to all who obey Him.

    Praise His name forever!

Proverbs 24

Don't envy evil people; don't desire their company. ²For they spend their days plotting violence, and their words are always stirring up trouble.

³A house is built by wisdom and becomes strong through good sense. ⁴Through knowledge its rooms are filled with all sorts of precious riches and valuables.

⁵A wise man is mightier than a strong man, and a man of knowledge is more powerful than a strong man. ⁶So

don't go to war without wise guidance; victory depends on having many counselors.

[7]Wisdom is too much for a fool. When the leaders gather, the fool has nothing to say.

[8]A person who plans evil will get a reputation as a troublemaker. [9]The schemes of a fool are sinful; everyone despises a mocker.

[10]If you fail under pressure, your strength is not very great.

[11]Rescue those who are unjustly sentenced to death; don't stand back and let them die. [12]Don't try to avoid responsibility by saying you didn't know about it. For God knows all hearts, and He sees you. He keeps watch over your soul, and He knows you knew! And He will judge all people according to what they have done.

[13]My child, eat honey, for it is good, and the honeycomb is sweet to the taste. [14]In the same way, wisdom is sweet to your soul. If you find it, you will have a bright future, and your hopes will not be cut short.

[15]Do not lie in wait like an outlaw at the home of the godly. And don't raid the house where the godly live. [16]They may trip seven times, but each time they will rise again. But one calamity is enough to lay the wicked low.

[17]Do not rejoice when your enemies fall into trouble. Don't be happy when they stumble. [18]For the LORD will be displeased with you and will turn His anger away from them.

¹⁹Do not fret because of evildoers; don't envy the wicked. ²⁰For the evil have no future; their light will be snuffed out.

²¹My child, fear the LORD and the king, and don't associate with rebels. ²²For you will go down with them to sudden disaster. Who knows where the punishment from the LORD and the king will end?

²³Here are some further sayings of the wise:

It is wrong to show favoritism when passing judgment. ²⁴A judge who says to the wicked, "You are innocent," will be cursed by many people and denounced by the nations. ²⁵But blessings are showered on those who convict the guilty.

²⁶It is an honor to receive an honest reply.

²⁷Develop your business first before building your house.

²⁸Do not testify spitefully against innocent neighbors; don't lie about them. ²⁹And don't say, "Now I can pay them back for all their meanness to me! I'll get even!"

³⁰I walked by the field of a lazy person, the vineyard of one lacking sense. ³¹I saw that it was overgrown with thorns. It was covered with weeds, and its walls were broken down. ³²Then, as I looked and thought about it, I learned this lesson: ³³A little extra sleep, a little more slumber, a little folding of the hands to rest—³⁴and poverty will pounce on you like a bandit; scarcity will attack you like an armed robber.

Notes

_____

_____

_____

_____

_____

_____

_____

_____

_____

_____

_____

_____

_____

_____

_____

_____

_____

_____

_____

_____

_____

_____

Psalm 112

¹ Praise the LORD!

Happy are those who fear the LORD.
   Yes, happy are those who delight in doing what He
      commands.
² Their children will be successful everywhere;
   an entire generation of godly people will be
      blessed.
³ They themselves will be wealthy,
   and their good deeds will never be forgotten.
⁴ When darkness overtakes the godly, light will come
      bursting in.
   They are generous, compassionate, and righteous.
⁵ All goes well for those who are generous,
   who lend freely and conduct their business fairly.
⁶ Such people will not be overcome by evil circumstances.
   Those who are righteous will be long remembered.
⁷ They do not fear bad news;
   they confidently trust the LORD to care for them.
⁸ They are confident and fearless
   and can face their foes triumphantly.

⁹ They give generously to those in need.
    Their good deeds will never be forgotten.
    They will have influence and honor.
¹⁰ The wicked will be infuriated when they
        see this.
    They will grind their teeth in anger;
    they will slink away, their hopes thwarted.

Psalm 113

¹ Praise the LORD!

  Yes, give praise, O servants of the LORD.
    Praise the name of the LORD!
² Blessed be the name of the LORD
    forever and ever.
³ Everywhere—from east to west—
    praise the name of the LORD.
⁴ For the LORD is high above the nations;
    His glory is far greater than the heavens.

⁵ Who can be compared with the LORD
        our God,
    who is enthroned on high?
⁶ Far below Him are the heavens and the earth.
    He stoops to look,

⁷ and He lifts the poor from the dirt
   and the needy from the garbage dump.
⁸ He sets them among princes,
   even the princes of His own people!
⁹ He gives the barren woman a home,
   so that she becomes a happy mother.

Praise the LORD!

Psalm 114

¹ When the Israelites escaped from Egypt—
   when the family of Jacob left that foreign land—
² the land of Judah became God's sanctuary,
   and Israel became His kingdom.

³ The Red Sea saw them coming and hurried out of their
      way!
   The water of the Jordan River turned away.
⁴ The mountains skipped like rams,
   the little hills like lambs!
⁵ What's wrong, Red Sea, that made you hurry out of
      their way?
   What happened, Jordan River, that you turned away?
⁶ Why, mountains, did you skip like rams?
   Why, little hills, like lambs?

⁷ Tremble, O earth, at the presence of the Lord,
   at the presence of the God of Israel.
⁸ He turned the rock into pools of water;
   yes, springs of water came from solid rock.

Psalm 115

¹ Not to us, O LORD, but to You goes all the glory
   for Your unfailing love and faithfulness.
² Why let the nations say,
   "Where is their God?"
³ For our God is in the heavens,
   and He does as He wishes.
⁴ Their idols are merely things of silver and gold,
   shaped by human hands.
⁵ They cannot talk, though they have mouths,
   or see, though they have eyes!
⁶ They cannot hear with their ears,
   or smell with their noses,
⁷   or feel with their hands,
   or walk with their feet,
   or utter sounds with their throats!
⁸ And those who make them are just like
      them,
   as are all who trust in them.

⁹O Israel, trust the LORD!
  He is your helper; He is your shield.
¹⁰O priests of Aaron, trust the LORD!
  He is your helper; He is your shield.
¹¹All you who fear the LORD, trust the LORD!
  He is your helper; He is your shield.

¹²The LORD remembers us,
    and He will surely bless us.
  He will bless the people of Israel
    and the family of Aaron, the priests.
¹³He will bless those who fear the LORD,
    both great and small.

¹⁴May the LORD richly bless
    both you and your children.
¹⁵May you be blessed by the LORD,
    who made heaven and earth.
¹⁶The heavens belong to the LORD,
    but He has given the earth to all
        humanity.

¹⁷The dead cannot sing praises to the LORD,
    for they have gone into the silence of
        the grave.
¹⁸But we can praise the LORD
    both now and forever!

  Praise the LORD!

Psalm 116

¹ I love the LORD because He hears
   and answers my prayers.
² Because He bends down and listens,
   I will pray as long as I have breath!
³ Death had its hands around my throat;
   the terrors of the grave overtook me.
   I saw only trouble and sorrow.
⁴ Then I called on the name of the LORD:
   "Please, LORD, save me!"
⁵ How kind the LORD is! How good He is!
   So merciful, this God of ours!
⁶ The LORD protects those of childlike
      faith;
   I was facing death, and then He saved me.
⁷ Now I can rest again,
   for the LORD has been so good to me.
⁸ He has saved me from death,
   my eyes from tears,
   my feet from stumbling.
⁹ And so I walk in the LORD's presence
   as I live here on earth!
¹⁰ I believed in You, so I prayed,
   "I am deeply troubled, LORD."
¹¹ In my anxiety I cried out to You,
   "These people are all liars!"

¹² What can I offer the LORD
   for all He has done for me?
¹³ I will lift up a cup symbolizing His salvation;
   I will praise the LORD's name for saving me.
¹⁴ I will keep my promises to the LORD
   in the presence of all His people.

¹⁵ The LORD's loved ones are precious to Him;
   it grieves Him when they die.
¹⁶ O LORD, I am Your servant;
   yes, I am Your servant, the son of Your
      handmaid,
   and You have freed me from my bonds!
¹⁷ I will offer You a sacrifice of thanksgiving
   and call on the name of the LORD.
¹⁸ I will keep my promises to the LORD
   in the presence of all His people,
¹⁹ in the house of the LORD,
   in the heart of Jerusalem.

   Praise the LORD!

Psalm 117

¹ Praise the LORD, all you nations.
   Praise Him, all you people of the earth.

² For He loves us with unfailing love;
the faithfulness of the LORD endures forever.

Praise the LORD!

Psalm 118

¹ Give thanks to the LORD, for He is good!
His faithful love endures forever.

² Let the congregation of Israel repeat:
"His faithful love endures forever."
³ Let Aaron's descendants, the priests, repeat:
"His faithful love endures forever."
⁴ Let all who fear the LORD repeat:
"His faithful love endures forever."

⁵ In my distress I prayed to the LORD,
and the LORD answered me and rescued me.
⁶ The LORD is for me, so I will not be afraid.
What can mere mortals do to me?
⁷ Yes, the LORD is for me; He will help me.
I will look in triumph at those who hate me.
⁸ It is better to trust the LORD
than to put confidence in people.
⁹ It is better to trust the LORD
than to put confidence in princes.

¹⁰ Though hostile nations surrounded me,
   I destroyed them all in the name of
      the LORD.
¹¹ Yes, they surrounded and attacked me,
   but I destroyed them all in the name of
      the LORD.
¹² They swarmed around me like bees;
   they blazed against me like a roaring
      flame.
   But I destroyed them all in the name of
      the LORD.
¹³ You did your best to kill me, O my enemy,
   but the LORD helped me.
¹⁴ The LORD is my strength and my song;
   He has become my victory.
¹⁵ Songs of joy and victory are sung in the camp of
      the godly.
   The strong right arm of the LORD has done
      glorious things!
¹⁶ The strong right arm of the LORD is raised
      in triumph.
   The strong right arm of the LORD has done
      glorious things!
¹⁷ I will not die, but I will live
   to tell what the LORD has done.
¹⁸ The LORD has punished me severely,
   but He has not handed me over to death.

¹⁹ Open for me the gates where the righteous
        enter,
    and I will go in and thank the LORD.
²⁰ Those gates lead to the presence of
        the LORD,
    and the godly enter there.
²¹ I thank You for answering my prayer
        and saving me!

²² The stone rejected by the builders
        has now become the cornerstone.
²³ This is the LORD's doing,
        and it is marvelous to see.
²⁴ This is the day the LORD has made.
        We will rejoice and be glad in it.
²⁵ Please, LORD, please save us.
        Please, LORD, please give us success.
²⁶ Bless the one who comes in the name of
        the LORD.
    We bless you from the house of the LORD.
²⁷ The LORD is God, shining upon us.
        Bring forward the sacrifice and put it
        on the altar.
²⁸ You are my God, and I will praise You!
        You are my God, and I will exalt You!

²⁹ Give thanks to the LORD, for He is good!
        His faithful love endures forever.

Proverbs 25

These are more proverbs of Solomon, collected by the advisers of King Hezekiah of Judah.

²It is God's privilege to conceal things and the king's privilege to discover them.

³No one can discover the height of heaven, the depth of the earth, or all that goes on in the king's mind!

⁴Remove the dross from silver, and the sterling will be ready for the silversmith. ⁵Remove the wicked from the king's court, and his reign will be made secure by justice.

⁶Don't demand an audience with the king or push for a place among the great. ⁷It is better to wait for an invitation than to be sent to the end of the line, publicly disgraced!

Just because you see something, ⁸don't be in a hurry to go to court. You might go down before your neighbors in shameful defeat. ⁹So discuss the matter with them privately. Don't tell anyone else, ¹⁰or others may accuse you of gossip. Then you will never regain your good reputation.

¹¹Timely advice is as lovely as golden apples in a silver basket.

¹²Valid criticism is as treasured by the one who heeds it as jewelry made from finest gold.

¹³Faithful messengers are as refreshing as snow in the heat of summer. They revive the spirit of their employer.

¹⁴A person who doesn't give a promised gift is like clouds and wind that don't bring rain.

¹⁵Patience can persuade a prince, and soft speech can crush strong opposition.

¹⁶Do you like honey? Don't eat too much of it, or it will make you sick!

¹⁷Don't visit your neighbors too often, or you will wear out your welcome.

¹⁸Telling lies about others is as harmful as hitting them with an ax, wounding them with a sword, or shooting them with a sharp arrow.

¹⁹Putting confidence in an unreliable person is like chewing with a toothache or walking on a broken foot.

²⁰Singing cheerful songs to a person whose heart is heavy is as bad as stealing someone's jacket in cold weather or rubbing salt in a wound.

²¹If your enemies are hungry, give them food to eat. If they are thirsty, give them water to drink. ²²You will heap burning coals on their heads, and the LORD will reward you.

²³As surely as a wind from the north brings rain, so a gossiping tongue causes anger!

²⁴It is better to live alone in the corner of an attic than with a contentious wife in a lovely home.

²⁵Good news from far away is like cold water to the thirsty.

²⁶If the godly compromise with the wicked, it is like polluting a fountain or muddying a spring.

[27]Just as it is not good to eat too much honey, it is not good for people to think about all the honors they deserve.

[28]A person without self-control is as defenseless as a city with broken-down walls.

Notes

_____

_____

_____

_____

_____

_____

_____

_____

_____

_____

_____

_____

Psalm 119

¹ Happy are people of integrity,
   who follow the law of the LORD.
² Happy are those who obey His decrees
   and search for Him with all their hearts.
³ They do not compromise with evil,
   and they walk only in His paths.
⁴ You have charged us
   to keep Your commandments carefully.
⁵ Oh, that my actions would consistently
   reflect Your principles!
⁶ Then I will not be disgraced
   when I compare my life with Your
     commands.
⁷ When I learn Your righteous laws,
   I will thank You by living as I should!
⁸ I will obey Your principles.
   Please don't give up on me!

⁹ How can a young person stay pure?
   By obeying Your word and following
     its rules.

¹⁰ I have tried my best to find You—
        don't let me wander from Your
            commands.
¹¹ I have hidden Your word in my heart,
        that I might not sin against You.
¹² Blessed are You, O LORD;
        teach me Your principles.
¹³ I have recited aloud
        all the laws You have given us.
¹⁴ I have rejoiced in Your decrees
        as much as in riches.
¹⁵ I will study Your commandments
        and reflect on Your ways.
¹⁶ I will delight in Your principles
        and not forget Your word.

¹⁷ Be good to Your servant,
        that I may live and obey Your word.
¹⁸ Open my eyes to see
        the wonderful truths in Your law.
¹⁹ I am but a foreigner here on earth;
        I need the guidance of Your commands.
        Don't hide them from me!
²⁰ I am overwhelmed continually
        with a desire for Your laws.
²¹ You rebuke those cursed proud ones
        who wander from Your commands.

²² Don't let them scorn and insult me,
>   for I have obeyed Your decrees.
²³ Even princes sit and speak against me,
>   but I will meditate on Your principles.
²⁴ Your decrees please me;
>   they give me wise advice.

²⁵ I lie in the dust, completely discouraged;
>   revive me by Your word.
²⁶ I told You my plans, and You answered.
>   Now teach me Your principles.
²⁷ Help me understand the meaning of Your
>   commandments,
>   and I will meditate on Your wonderful
>   miracles.
²⁸ I weep with grief;
>   encourage me by Your word.
²⁹ Keep me from lying to myself;
>   give me the privilege of knowing Your law.
³⁰ I have chosen to be faithful;
>   I have determined to live by Your laws.
³¹ I cling to Your decrees.
>   LORD, don't let me be put to shame!
³² If You will help me,
>   I will run to follow Your commands.

³³ Teach me, O LORD,
>   to follow every one of Your principles.

³⁴ Give me understanding and I will obey Your law;
    I will put it into practice with all my heart.
³⁵ Make me walk along the path of Your commands,
    for that is where my happiness is found.
³⁶ Give me an eagerness for Your decrees;
    do not inflict me with love for money!
³⁷ Turn my eyes from worthless things,
    and give me life through Your word.
³⁸ Reassure me of Your promise,
    which is for those who honor You.
³⁹ Help me abandon my shameful ways;
    Your laws are all I want in life.
⁴⁰ I long to obey Your commandments!
    Renew my life with Your goodness.

⁴¹ LORD, give to me Your unfailing love,
    the salvation that You promised me.
⁴² Then I will have an answer for those who taunt me,
    for I trust in Your word.
⁴³ Do not snatch Your word of truth from me,
    for my only hope is in Your laws.
⁴⁴ I will keep on obeying Your law
    forever and forever.
⁴⁵ I will walk in freedom,
    for I have devoted myself to Your commandments.
⁴⁶ I will speak to kings about Your decrees,
    and I will not be ashamed.

⁴⁷ How I delight in Your commands!
    How I love them!
⁴⁸ I honor and love Your commands.
    I meditate on Your principles.

⁴⁹ Remember Your promise to me,
    for it is my only hope.
⁵⁰ Your promise revives me;
    it comforts me in all my troubles.
⁵¹ The proud hold me in utter contempt,
    but I do not turn away from Your law.
⁵² I meditate on Your age-old laws;
    O LORD, they comfort me.
⁵³ I am furious with the wicked,
    those who reject Your law.
⁵⁴ Your principles have been the music of my life
    throughout the years of my pilgrimage.
⁵⁵ I reflect at night on who You are, O LORD,
    and I obey Your law because of this.
⁵⁶ This is my happy way of life:
    obeying Your commandments.

⁵⁷ LORD, You are mine!
    I promise to obey Your words!
⁵⁸ With all my heart I want Your blessings.
    Be merciful just as You promised.
⁵⁹ I pondered the direction of my life,
    and I turned to follow Your statutes.

⁶⁰ I will hurry, without lingering,
    to obey Your commands.
⁶¹ Evil people try to drag me into sin,
    but I am firmly anchored to Your law.
⁶² At midnight I rise to thank You
    for Your just laws.
⁶³ Anyone who fears You is my friend—
    anyone who obeys Your commandments.
⁶⁴ O LORD, the earth is full of Your unfailing love;
    teach me Your principles.

⁶⁵ You have done many good things for me, LORD,
    just as You promised.
⁶⁶ I believe in Your commands;
    now teach me good judgment and knowledge.
⁶⁷ I used to wander off until You disciplined me;
    but now I closely follow Your word.
⁶⁸ You are good and do only good;
    teach me Your principles.
⁶⁹ Arrogant people have made up lies about me,
    but in truth I obey Your commandments with all my
        heart.
⁷⁰ Their hearts are dull and stupid,
    but I delight in Your law.
⁷¹ The suffering You sent was good for me,
    for it taught me to pay attention to Your
        principles.

⁷² Your law is more valuable to me
     than millions in gold and silver!

⁷³ You made me; You created me.
     Now give me the sense to follow Your commands.
⁷⁴ May all who fear You find in me a cause for joy,
     for I have put my hope in Your word.
⁷⁵ I know, O LORD, that Your decisions are fair;
     You disciplined me because I needed it.
⁷⁶ Now let Your unfailing love comfort me,
     just as You promised me, Your servant.
⁷⁷ Surround me with Your tender mercies so
      I may live,
     for Your law is my delight.
⁷⁸ Bring disgrace upon the arrogant people who
      lied about me;
     meanwhile, I will concentrate on Your
      commandments.
⁷⁹ Let me be reconciled
     with all who fear You and know Your decrees.
⁸⁰ May I be blameless in keeping Your principles;
     then I will never have to be ashamed.

⁸¹ I faint with longing for Your salvation;
     but I have put my hope in Your word.
⁸² My eyes are straining to see Your promises
      come true.
     When will You comfort me?

⁸³ I am shriveled like a wineskin in the smoke, exhausted
    with waiting.

  But I cling to Your principles and obey them.
⁸⁴ How long must I wait?

  When will You punish those who persecute me?
⁸⁵ These arrogant people who hate Your law

  have dug deep pits for me to fall into.
⁸⁶ All Your commands are trustworthy.

  Protect me from those who hunt me down without
    cause.
⁸⁷ They almost finished me off,

  but I refused to abandon Your commandments.
⁸⁸ In Your unfailing love, spare my life;

  then I can continue to obey Your decrees.

⁸⁹ Forever, O LORD,

  Your word stands firm in heaven.
⁹⁰ Your faithfulness extends to every generation,

  as enduring as the earth You created.
⁹¹ Your laws remain true today,

  for everything serves Your plans.
⁹² If Your law hadn't sustained me with joy,

  I would have died in my misery.
⁹³ I will never forget Your commandments,

  for You have used them to restore my joy
    and health.
⁹⁴ I am Yours; save me!

For I have applied myself to obey Your
   commandments.
95 Though the wicked hide along the way to kill me,
   I will quietly keep my mind on Your decrees.
96 Even perfection has its limits,
   but Your commands have no limit.

97 Oh, how I love Your law!
   I think about it all day long.
98 Your commands make me wiser than my enemies,
   for Your commands are my constant guide.
99 Yes, I have more insight than my teachers,
   for I am always thinking of Your decrees.
100 I am even wiser than my elders,
   for I have kept Your commandments.
101 I have refused to walk on any path of evil,
   that I may remain obedient to Your word.
102 I haven't turned away from Your laws,
   for You have taught me well.
103 How sweet are Your words to my taste;
   they are sweeter than honey.
104 Your commandments give me understanding;
   no wonder I hate every false way of life.

105 Your word is a lamp for my feet
   and a light for my path.
106 I've promised it once, and I'll promise again:
   I will obey Your wonderful laws.

¹⁰⁷ I have suffered much, O LORD;
    restore my life again, just as You promised.
¹⁰⁸ LORD, accept my grateful thanks
    and teach me Your laws.
¹⁰⁹ My life constantly hangs in the balance,
    but I will not stop obeying Your law.
¹¹⁰ The wicked have set their traps for me along
        Your path,
    but I will not turn from Your commandments.
¹¹¹ Your decrees are my treasure;
    they are truly my heart's delight.
¹¹² I am determined to keep Your principles,
    even forever, to the very end.

¹¹³ I hate those who are undecided about You,
    but my choice is clear—I love Your law.
¹¹⁴ You are my refuge and my shield;
    Your word is my only source of hope.
¹¹⁵ Get out of my life, you evil-minded people,
    for I intend to obey the commands of
        my God.
¹¹⁶ LORD, sustain me as You promised, that I
        may live!
    Do not let my hope be crushed.
¹¹⁷ Sustain me, and I will be saved;
    then I will meditate on Your principles
        continually.

¹¹⁸ But You have rejected all who stray from Your
 principles.

 They are only fooling themselves.

¹¹⁹ All the wicked of the earth are the scum You
 skim off;

 no wonder I love to obey Your decrees!

¹²⁰ I tremble in fear of You;

 I fear Your judgments.

¹²¹ Don't leave me to the mercy of my enemies,

 for I have done what is just and right.

¹²² Please guarantee a blessing for me.

 Don't let those who are arrogant oppress me!

¹²³ My eyes strain to see Your deliverance,

 to see the truth of Your promise fulfilled.

¹²⁴ I am Your servant;

 deal with me in unfailing love,

 and teach me Your principles.

¹²⁵ Give discernment to me, Your servant;

 then I will understand Your decrees.

¹²⁶ LORD, it is time for You to act,

 for these evil people have broken
 Your law.

¹²⁷ Truly, I love Your commands

 more than gold, even the finest gold.

¹²⁸ Truly, each of Your commandments is right.

 That is why I hate every false way.

¹²⁹ Your decrees are wonderful.
No wonder I obey them!

¹³⁰ As Your words are taught, they give light;
even the simple can understand them.

¹³¹ I open my mouth, panting expectantly,
longing for Your commands.

¹³² Come and show me Your mercy,
as You do for all who love Your name.

¹³³ Guide my steps by Your word,
so I will not be overcome by any evil.

¹³⁴ Rescue me from the oppression of evil people;
then I can obey Your commandments.

¹³⁵ Look down on me with love;
teach me all Your principles.

¹³⁶ Rivers of tears gush from my eyes
because people disobey Your law.

¹³⁷ O LORD, You are righteous,
and Your decisions are fair.

¹³⁸ Your decrees are perfect;
they are entirely worthy of our trust.

¹³⁹ I am overwhelmed with rage,
for my enemies have disregarded Your words.

¹⁴⁰ Your promises have been thoroughly tested;
that is why I love them so much.

¹⁴¹ I am insignificant and despised,
but I don't forget Your commandments.

¹⁴² Your justice is eternal,
    and Your law is perfectly true.
¹⁴³ As pressure and stress bear down on me,
    I find joy in Your commands.
¹⁴⁴ Your decrees are always fair;
    help me to understand them, that I may live.

¹⁴⁵ I pray with all my heart; answer me, LORD!
    I will obey Your principles.
¹⁴⁶ I cry out to You; save me,
    that I may obey Your decrees.
¹⁴⁷ I rise early, before the sun is up;
    I cry out for help and put my hope in Your words.
¹⁴⁸ I stay awake through the night,
    thinking about Your promise.
¹⁴⁹ In Your faithful love, O LORD, hear my cry;
    in Your justice, save my life.
¹⁵⁰ Those lawless people are coming near to attack me;
    they live far from Your law.
¹⁵¹ But You are near, O LORD,
    and all Your commands are true.
¹⁵² I have known from my earliest days
    that Your decrees never change.

¹⁵³ Look down upon my sorrows and rescue me,
    for I have not forgotten Your law.
¹⁵⁴ Argue my case; take my side!
    Protect my life as You promised.

¹⁵⁵ The wicked are far from salvation,
    for they do not bother with Your principles.
¹⁵⁶ LORD, how great is Your mercy;
    in Your justice, give me back my life.
¹⁵⁷ Many persecute and trouble me,
    yet I have not swerved from Your decrees.
¹⁵⁸ I hate these traitors
    because they care nothing for Your word.
¹⁵⁹ See how I love Your commandments, LORD.
    Give back my life because of Your unfailing love.
¹⁶⁰ All Your words are true;
    all Your just laws will stand forever.

¹⁶¹ Powerful people harass me without cause,
    but my heart trembles only at Your word.
¹⁶² I rejoice in Your word
    like one who finds a great treasure.
¹⁶³ I hate and abhor all falsehood,
    but I love Your law.
¹⁶⁴ I will praise You seven times a day
    because all Your laws are just.
¹⁶⁵ Those who love Your law have great peace
    and do not stumble.
¹⁶⁶ I long for Your salvation, LORD,
    so I have obeyed Your commands.
¹⁶⁷ I have obeyed Your decrees,
    and I love them very much.

¹⁶⁸ Yes, I obey Your commandments and decrees,
  because You know everything I do.

¹⁶⁹ O LORD, listen to my cry;
  give me the discerning mind You promised.

¹⁷⁰ Listen to my prayer;
  rescue me as You promised.

¹⁷¹ Let my lips burst forth with praise,
  for You have taught me Your principles.

¹⁷² Let my tongue sing about Your word,
  for all Your commands are right.

¹⁷³ Stand ready to help me,
  for I have chosen to follow Your
    commandments.

¹⁷⁴ O LORD, I have longed for Your salvation,
  and Your law is my delight.

¹⁷⁵ Let me live so I can praise You,
  and may Your laws sustain me.

¹⁷⁶ I have wandered away like a lost sheep;
  come and find me,
  for I have not forgotten Your commands.

Proverbs 26

Honor doesn't go with fools any more than snow with
summer or rain with harvest.

²Like a fluttering sparrow or a darting swallow, an unfair curse will not land on its intended victim.

³Guide a horse with a whip, a donkey with a bridle, and a fool with a rod to his back!

⁴When arguing with fools, don't answer their foolish arguments, or you will become as foolish as they are.

⁵When arguing with fools, be sure to answer their foolish arguments, or they will become wise in their own estimation.

⁶Trusting a fool to convey a message is as foolish as cutting off one's feet or drinking poison!

⁷In the mouth of a fool, a proverb becomes as limp as a paralyzed leg.

⁸Honoring a fool is as foolish as tying a stone to a slingshot.

⁹A proverb in a fool's mouth is as dangerous as a thornbush brandished by a drunkard.

¹⁰An employer who hires a fool or a bystander is like an archer who shoots recklessly.

¹¹As a dog returns to its vomit, so a fool repeats his folly.

¹²There is more hope for fools than for people who think they are wise.

¹³The lazy person is full of excuses, saying, "I can't go outside because there might be a lion on the road! Yes, I'm sure there's a lion out there!"

¹⁴As a door turns back and forth on its hinges, so the lazy person turns over in bed.

¹⁵Some people are so lazy that they won't lift a finger to feed themselves.

¹⁶Lazy people consider themselves smarter than seven wise counselors.

¹⁷Yanking a dog's ears is as foolish as interfering in someone else's argument.

¹⁸Just as damaging as a mad man shooting a lethal weapon ¹⁹is someone who lies to a friend and then says, "I was only joking."

²⁰Fire goes out for lack of fuel, and quarrels disappear when gossip stops.

²¹A quarrelsome person starts fights as easily as hot embers light charcoal or fire lights wood.

²²What dainty morsels rumors are—but they sink deep into one's heart.

²³Smooth words may hide a wicked heart, just as a pretty glaze covers a common clay pot.

²⁴People with hate in their hearts may sound pleasant enough, but don't believe them. ²⁵Though they pretend to be kind, their hearts are full of all kinds of evil. ²⁶While their hatred may be concealed by trickery, it will finally come to light for all to see.

²⁷If you set a trap for others, you will get caught in it yourself. If you roll a boulder down on others, it will roll back and crush you.

²⁸A lying tongue hates its victims, and flattery causes ruin.

Notes

_____

_____

_____

_____

_____

_____

_____

_____

_____

_____

_____

_____

_____

_____

_____

_____

_____

_____

_____

Psalm 120

A song for the ascent to Jerusalem.

¹ I took my troubles to the LORD;
   I cried out to Him, and He answered
     my prayer.
² Rescue me, O LORD, from liars
   and from all deceitful people.
³ O deceptive tongue, what will God do
     to you?
   How will He increase your punishment?
⁴ You will be pierced with sharp arrows
   and burned with glowing coals.

⁵ How I suffer among these scoundrels of
     Meshech!
   It pains me to live with these people from
     Kedar!
⁶ I am tired of living here
   among people who hate peace.
⁷ As for me, I am for peace;
   but when I speak, they are for war!

Psalm 121

A song for the ascent to Jerusalem.

¹ I look up to the mountains—
   does my help come from there?
² My help comes from the LORD,
   who made the heavens and the earth!

³ He will not let you stumble and fall;
   the One who watches over you will not sleep.
⁴ Indeed, He who watches over Israel
   never tires and never sleeps.

⁵ The LORD Himself watches over you!
   The LORD stands beside you as your protective shade.
⁶ The sun will not hurt you by day,
   nor the moon at night.
⁷ The LORD keeps you from all evil
   and preserves your life.
⁸ The LORD keeps watch over you as you come and go,
   both now and forever.

Psalm 122

A song for the ascent to Jerusalem. A psalm of David.

¹ I was glad when they said to me,
   "Let us go to the house of the LORD."

² And now we are standing here
  inside your gates, O Jerusalem.
³ Jerusalem is a well-built city,
  knit together as a single unit.
⁴ All the people of Israel—the LORD's people—
  make their pilgrimage here.
 They come to give thanks to the name of
   the LORD
  as the law requires.
⁵ Here stand the thrones where judgment is given,
  the thrones of the dynasty of David.

⁶ Pray for the peace of Jerusalem.
  May all who love this city prosper.
⁷ O Jerusalem, may there be peace within your walls
  and prosperity in your palaces.
⁸ For the sake of my family and friends, I will say,
  "Peace be with you."
⁹ For the sake of the house of the LORD our God,
  I will seek what is best for you, O Jerusalem.

Psalm 123

A song for the ascent to Jerusalem.

¹ I lift my eyes to You,
  O God, enthroned in heaven.

²We look to the LORD our God for His mercy,
>just as servants keep their eyes on their
>>master,
>as a slave girl watches her mistress for the
>>slightest signal.

³Have mercy on us, LORD, have mercy,
>for we have had our fill of contempt.
⁴We have had our fill of the scoffing of the
>>proud
>and the contempt of the arrogant.

Psalm 124

A song for the ascent to Jerusalem. A psalm of David.

¹If the LORD had not been on our side—
>let Israel now say—
²if the LORD had not been on our side
>when people rose up against us,
³they would have swallowed us alive
>because of their burning anger against us.
⁴The waters would have engulfed us;
>a torrent would have overwhelmed us.
⁵Yes, the raging waters of their fury
>would have overwhelmed our very lives.

⁶ Blessed be the LORD,

    who did not let their teeth tear us apart!

⁷ We escaped like a bird from a hunter's trap.

    The trap is broken, and we are free!

⁸ Our help is from the LORD,

    who made the heavens and the earth.

Psalm 125

A song for the ascent to Jerusalem.

¹ Those who trust in the LORD are as secure as

    Mount Zion;

    they will not be defeated but will endure forever.

² Just as the mountains surround and protect

    Jerusalem,

    so the LORD surrounds and protects His people,

    both now and forever.

³ The wicked will not rule the godly,

    for then the godly might be forced to do wrong.

⁴ O LORD, do good to those who are good,

    whose hearts are in tune with You.

⁵ But banish those who turn to crooked ways,

    O LORD.

    Take them away with those who do evil.

    And let Israel have quietness and peace.

Psalm 126

A song for the ascent to Jerusalem.

¹ When the LORD restored His exiles to Jerusalem,
   it was like a dream!
² We were filled with laughter,
   and we sang for joy.
 And the other nations said,
   "What amazing things the LORD has done for them."
³ Yes, the LORD has done amazing things for us!
   What joy!

⁴ Restore our fortunes, LORD,
   as streams renew the desert.
⁵ Those who plant in tears
   will harvest with shouts of joy.
⁶ They weep as they go to plant their seed,
   but they sing as they return with the harvest.

Psalm 127

A song for the ascent to Jerusalem. A psalm of Solomon.

¹ Unless the LORD builds a house,
   the work of the builders is useless.
 Unless the LORD protects a city,
   guarding it with sentries will do no good.

² It is useless for you to work so hard
    from early morning until late at night,
  anxiously working for food to eat;
      for God gives rest to His loved ones.

³ Children are a gift from the LORD;
    they are a reward from Him.
⁴ Children born to a young man
    are like sharp arrows in a warrior's hands.
⁵ How happy is the man whose quiver is full of them!
      He will not be put to shame when he confronts his
      accusers at the city gates.

Psalm 128

A song for the ascent to Jerusalem.

¹ How happy are those who fear the LORD—
    all who follow His ways!
² You will enjoy the fruit of your labor.
    How happy you will be! How rich
      your life!
³ Your wife will be like a fruitful vine,
    flourishing within your home.
  And look at all those children!
    There they sit around your table
    as vigorous and healthy as young olive trees.

⁴ That is the LORD's reward
  for those who fear Him.

⁵ May the LORD continually bless you from Zion.
  May you see Jerusalem prosper as long as you live.
⁶ May you live to enjoy your grandchildren.
  And may Israel have quietness and peace.

Psalm 129

A song for the ascent to Jerusalem.

¹ From my earliest youth my enemies have persecuted me—
  let Israel now say—
² from my earliest youth my enemies have persecuted me,
  but they have never been able to finish me off.
³ My back is covered with cuts,
  as if a farmer had plowed long furrows.
⁴ But the LORD is good;
  He has cut the cords used by the ungodly to bind me.

⁵ May all who hate Jerusalem
  be turned back in shameful defeat.
⁶ May they be as useless as grass on a rooftop,
  turning yellow when only half grown,
⁷   ignored by the harvester,
  despised by the binder.

⁸ And may those who pass by refuse to give them this
      blessing:
    "The LORD's blessings be upon you;
    we bless you in the LORD's name."

Proverbs 27

Don't brag about tomorrow, since you don't know what
the day will bring.

²Don't praise yourself; let others do it!

³A stone is heavy and sand is weighty, but the resentment caused by a fool is heavier than both.

⁴Anger is cruel, and wrath is like a flood, but who can survive the destructiveness of jealousy?

⁵An open rebuke is better than hidden love!

⁶Wounds from a friend are better than many kisses from an enemy.

⁷Honey seems tasteless to a person who is full, but even bitter food tastes sweet to the hungry.

⁸A person who strays from home is like a bird that strays from its nest.

⁹The heartfelt counsel of a friend is as sweet as perfume and incense.

¹⁰Never abandon a friend—either yours or your father's. Then in your time of need, you won't have to ask your

relatives for assistance. It is better to go to a neighbor than to a relative who lives far away.

[11]My child, how happy I will be if you turn out to be wise! Then I will be able to answer my critics.

[12]A prudent person foresees the danger ahead and takes precautions. The simpleton goes blindly on and suffers the consequences.

[13]Be sure to get collateral from anyone who guarantees the debt of a stranger. Get a deposit if someone guarantees the debt of an adulterous woman.

[14]If you shout a pleasant greeting to your neighbor too early in the morning, it will be counted as a curse!

[15]A nagging wife is as annoying as the constant dripping on a rainy day. [16]Trying to stop her complaints is like trying to stop the wind or hold something with greased hands.

[17]As iron sharpens iron, a friend sharpens a friend.

[18]Workers who tend a fig tree are allowed to eat its fruit. In the same way, workers who protect their employer's interests will be rewarded.

[19]As a face is reflected in water, so the heart reflects the person.

[20]Just as Death and Destruction are never satisfied, so human desire is never satisfied.

[21]Fire tests the purity of silver and gold, but a person is tested by being praised.

[22]You cannot separate fools from their foolishness, even though you grind them like grain with mortar and pestle.

[23]Know the state of your flocks, and put your heart into caring for your herds, [24]for riches don't last forever, and the crown might not be secure for the next generation. [25]After the hay is harvested, the new crop appears, and the mountain grasses are gathered in, [26]your sheep will provide wool for clothing, and your goats will be sold for the price of a field. [27]And you will have enough goats' milk for you, your family, and your servants.

Notes

_____

_____

_____

_____

_____

_____

_____

_____

_____

_____

_____

Psalm 130

A song for the ascent to Jerusalem.

¹ From the depths of despair, O LORD,
  I call for Your help.
² Hear my cry, O Lord.
  Pay attention to my prayer.

³ LORD, if You kept a record of our sins,
  who, O Lord, could ever survive?
⁴ But You offer forgiveness,
  that we might learn to fear You.

⁵ I am counting on the LORD;
  yes, I am counting on Him.
  I have put my hope in His word.
⁶ I long for the Lord
  more than sentries long for the dawn,
  yes, more than sentries long for the dawn.

⁷ O Israel, hope in the LORD;
  for with the LORD there is unfailing love
  and an overflowing supply of salvation.
⁸ He Himself will free Israel
  from every kind of sin.

Psalm 131

A song for the ascent to Jerusalem. A psalm of David.

¹ LORD, my heart is not proud;
   my eyes are not haughty.
 I don't concern myself with matters too great
   or awesome for me.
² But I have stilled and quieted myself,
   just as a small child is quiet with its mother.
   Yes, like a small child is my soul within me.

³ O Israel, put your hope in the LORD—
   now and always.

Psalm 132

A song for the ascent to Jerusalem.

¹ LORD, remember David
   and all that he suffered.
² He took an oath before the LORD.
   He vowed to the Mighty One of Israel,
³ "I will not go home;
   I will not let myself rest.
⁴ I will not let my eyes sleep
   nor close my eyelids in slumber
⁵   until I find a place to build a house for the LORD,
   a sanctuary for the Mighty One of Israel."

⁶ We heard that the Ark was in Ephrathah;
   then we found it in the distant countryside of Jaar.
⁷ Let us go to the dwelling place of the LORD;
   let us bow low before Him.
⁸ Arise, O LORD, and enter Your sanctuary,
   along with the Ark, the symbol of Your power.
⁹ Your priests will be agents of salvation;
   may Your loyal servants sing for joy.

¹⁰ For the sake of Your servant David,
   do not reject the king You chose for Your people.
¹¹ The LORD swore to David
   a promise He will never take back:
  "I will place one of your descendants on your throne.
¹² If your descendants obey the terms of My covenant
   and follow the decrees that I teach them,
  then your royal line will never end."

¹³ For the LORD has chosen Jerusalem;
   He has desired it as his home.
¹⁴ "This is My home where I will live forever," He said.
   "I will live here, for this is the place I desired.
¹⁵ I will make this city prosperous
   and satisfy its poor with food.
¹⁶ I will make its priests the agents of salvation;
   its godly people will sing for joy.
¹⁷ Here I will increase the power of David;
   My anointed one will be a light for My people.

¹⁸ I will clothe his enemies with shame,
    but he will be a glorious king."

Psalm 133

A song for the ascent to Jerusalem. A psalm of David.

¹ How wonderful it is, how pleasant,
    when brothers live together in harmony!
² For harmony is as precious as the fragrant anointing oil
    that was poured over Aaron's head,
    that ran down his beard
    and onto the border of his robe.
³ Harmony is as refreshing as the dew from Mount
        Hermon
    that falls on the mountains of Zion.
And the LORD has pronounced His blessing,
    even life forevermore.

Psalm 134

A song for the ascent to Jerusalem.

¹ Oh, bless the LORD, all you servants of the LORD,
    you who serve as night watchmen in the house of the
        LORD.

² Lift your hands in holiness,
　　and bless the LORD.

³ May the LORD, who made heaven and earth,
　　bless you from Jerusalem.

Proverbs 28

The wicked run away when no one is chasing them, but the godly are as bold as lions.

²When there is moral rot within a nation, its government topples easily. But with wise and knowledgeable leaders, there is stability.

³A poor person who oppresses the poor is like a pounding rain that destroys the crops.

⁴To reject the law is to praise the wicked; to obey the law is to fight them.

⁵Evil people don't understand justice, but those who follow the LORD understand completely.

⁶It is better to be poor and honest than rich and crooked.

⁷Young people who obey the law are wise; those who seek out worthless companions bring shame to their parents.

⁸A person who makes money by charging interest will lose it. It will end up in the hands of someone who is kind to the poor.

⁹The prayers of a person who ignores the law are despised.

¹⁰Those who lead the upright into sin will fall into their own trap, but the honest will inherit good things.

¹¹Rich people picture themselves as wise, but their real poverty is evident to the poor.

¹²When the godly succeed, everyone is glad. When the wicked take charge, people go into hiding.

¹³People who cover over their sins will not prosper. But if they confess and forsake them, they will receive mercy.

¹⁴Blessed are those who have a tender conscience, but the stubborn are headed for serious trouble.

¹⁵A wicked ruler is as dangerous to the poor as a lion or bear attacking them.

¹⁶Only a stupid prince will oppress his people, but a king will have a long reign if he hates dishonesty and bribes.

¹⁷A murderer's tormented conscience will drive him into the grave. Don't protect him!

¹⁸The honest will be rescued from harm, but those who are crooked will be destroyed.

¹⁹Hard workers have plenty of food; playing around brings poverty.

²⁰The trustworthy will get a rich reward. But the person who wants to get rich quick will only get into trouble.

²¹Showing partiality is never good, yet some will do wrong for something as small as a piece of bread.

²²A greedy person tries to get rich quick, but it only leads to poverty.

²³In the end, people appreciate frankness more than flattery.

²⁴Robbing your parents and then saying, "What's wrong with that?" is as serious as committing murder.

²⁵Greed causes fighting; trusting the LORD leads to prosperity.

²⁶Trusting oneself is foolish, but those who walk in wisdom are safe.

²⁷Whoever gives to the poor will lack nothing. But a curse will come upon those who close their eyes to poverty.

²⁸When the wicked take charge, people hide. When the wicked meet disaster, the godly multiply.

Notes

Notes

Psalm 135

¹ Praise the LORD!

Praise the name of the LORD!
Praise Him, you who serve the LORD,
²   you who serve in the house of the LORD,
in the courts of the house of our God.
³ Praise the LORD, for the LORD is good;
celebrate His wonderful name with music.
⁴ For the LORD has chosen Jacob for Himself,
Israel for His own special treasure.

⁵ I know the greatness of the LORD—
that our Lord is greater than any other god.
⁶ The LORD does whatever pleases Him
throughout all heaven and earth,
and on the seas and in their depths.
⁷ He causes the clouds to rise over the earth.
He sends the lightning with the rain
and releases the wind from His storehouses.
⁸ He destroyed the firstborn in each Egyptian home,
both people and animals.

⁹ He performed miraculous signs and wonders
    in Egypt;
    Pharaoh and all his people watched.
¹⁰ He struck down great nations
    and slaughtered mighty kings—
¹¹   Sihon king of the Amorites,
    Og king of Bashan,
    and all the kings of Canaan.
¹² He gave their land as an inheritance,
    a special possession to His people Israel.
¹³ Your name, O LORD, endures forever;
    Your fame, O LORD, is known to every
      generation.
¹⁴ For the LORD will vindicate His people
    and have compassion on His servants.

¹⁵ Their idols are merely things of silver and gold,
    shaped by human hands.
¹⁶ They cannot talk, though they have mouths,
    or see, though they have eyes!
¹⁷ They cannot hear with their ears
    or smell with their noses.
¹⁸ And those who make them are just like
    them,
    as are all who trust in them.

¹⁹ O Israel, praise the LORD!
    O priests of Aaron, praise the LORD!

365

²⁰O Levites, praise the LORD!
   All you who fear the LORD, praise the LORD!
²¹The LORD be praised from Zion,
   for He lives here in Jerusalem.

  Praise the LORD!

Psalm 136

¹Give thanks to the LORD, for He is good!
          His faithful love endures forever.
²Give thanks to the God of gods.
          His faithful love endures forever.
³Give thanks to the Lord of lords.
          His faithful love endures forever.

⁴Give thanks to Him who alone does mighty miracles.
          His faithful love endures forever.
⁵Give thanks to Him who made the heavens so skillfully.
          His faithful love endures forever.
⁶Give thanks to Him who placed the earth on the water.
          His faithful love endures forever.
⁷Give thanks to Him who made the heavenly lights—
          His faithful love endures forever.
⁸ the sun to rule the day,
          His faithful love endures forever.

9   and the moon and stars to rule the night.

His faithful love endures forever.

10 Give thanks to Him who killed the firstborn of Egypt.

His faithful love endures forever.

11 He brought Israel out of Egypt.

His faithful love endures forever.

12 He acted with a strong hand and powerful arm.

His faithful love endures forever.

13 Give thanks to Him who parted the Red Sea.

His faithful love endures forever.

14 He led Israel safely through,

His faithful love endures forever.

15   but He hurled Pharaoh and his army into the sea.

His faithful love endures forever.

16 Give thanks to Him who led his people through the
        wilderness.   *His faithful love endures forever.*

17 Give thanks to Him who struck down mighty kings.

His faithful love endures forever.

18 He killed powerful kings—

His faithful love endures forever.

19   Sihon king of the Amorites,

His faithful love endures forever.

20   and Og king of Bashan.

His faithful love endures forever.

21 God gave the land of these kings as an inheritance—

His faithful love endures forever.

²²   a special possession to His servant Israel.
                    His faithful love endures forever.

²³ He remembered our utter weakness.
                    His faithful love endures forever.
²⁴ He saved us from our enemies.
                    His faithful love endures forever.
²⁵ He gives food to every living thing.
                    His faithful love endures forever.

²⁶ Give thanks to the God of heaven.
                    His faithful love endures forever.

Psalm 137

¹ Beside the rivers of Babylon, we sat and wept
    as we thought of Jerusalem.
² We put away our lyres,
    hanging them on the branches of the willow trees.
³ For there our captors demanded a song of us.
    Our tormentors requested a joyful hymn:
    "Sing us one of those songs of Jerusalem!"
⁴ But how can we sing the songs of the LORD
    while in a foreign land?

⁵ If I forget you, O Jerusalem,
    let my right hand forget its skill upon the harp.

⁶ May my tongue stick to the roof of my mouth
    if I fail to remember you,
    if I don't make Jerusalem my highest joy.

⁷ O LORD, remember what the Edomites did
    on the day the armies of Babylon captured Jerusalem.
  "Destroy it!" they yelled.
    "Level it to the ground!"
⁸ O Babylon, you will be destroyed.
    Happy is the one who pays you back
    for what you have done to us.
⁹ Happy is the one who takes your babies
    and smashes them against the rocks!

Psalm 138

A psalm of David.

¹ I give You thanks, O LORD, with all my heart;
    I will sing Your praises before the gods.
² I bow before Your holy Temple as I worship.
    I will give thanks to Your name
    for Your unfailing love and faithfulness,
  because Your promises are backed
    by all the honor of Your name.
³ When I pray, You answer me;
    You encourage me by giving me the strength I need.

⁴ Every king in all the earth will give You thanks, O LORD,
    for all of them will hear Your words.
⁵ Yes, they will sing about the LORD's ways,
    for the glory of the LORD is very great.
⁶ Though the LORD is great, He cares for the humble,
    but He keeps His distance from the proud.

⁷ Though I am surrounded by troubles,
    You will preserve me against the anger of my enemies.
 You will clench Your fist against my angry enemies!
    Your power will save me.
⁸ The LORD will work out His plans for my life—
    for Your faithful love, O LORD, endures forever.
    Don't abandon me, for You made me.

Psalm 139

For the choir director: A psalm of David.

¹ O LORD, You have examined my heart
    and know everything about me.
² You know when I sit down or stand up.
    You know my every thought when far away.
³ You chart the path ahead of me
    and tell me where to stop and rest.
    Every moment You know where I am.
⁴ You know what I am going to say
    even before I say it, LORD.

⁵ You both precede and follow me.
   You place Your hand of blessing on my head.
⁶ Such knowledge is too wonderful for me,
   too great for me to know!

⁷ I can never escape from Your Spirit!
   I can never get away from Your presence!
⁸ If I go up to heaven, You are there;
   if I go down to the place of the dead, You
      are there.
⁹ If I ride the wings of the morning,
   if I dwell by the farthest oceans,
¹⁰ even there Your hand will guide me,
   and Your strength will support me.
¹¹ I could ask the darkness to hide me
   and the light around me to become night—
¹² but even in darkness I cannot hide from You.
   To You the night shines as bright as day.
      Darkness and light are both alike to You.

¹³ You made all the delicate, inner parts of my body
   and knit me together in my mother's womb.
¹⁴ Thank You for making me so wonderfully complex!
   Your workmanship is marvelous—and how well I
      know it.
¹⁵ You watched me as I was being formed in utter
      seclusion,
   as I was woven together in the dark of the womb.

¹⁶ You saw me before I was born.
>> Every day of my life was recorded in
>>> Your book.
>> Every moment was laid out
>>> before a single day had passed.

¹⁷ How precious are Your thoughts about me,
>>> O God!
>> They are innumerable!
¹⁸ I can't even count them;
>> they outnumber the grains of sand!
> And when I wake up in the morning,
>> You are still with me!

¹⁹ O God, if only You would destroy the
>>> wicked!
>> Get out of my life, you murderers!
²⁰ They blaspheme You;
>> Your enemies take Your name in vain.
²¹ O Lord, shouldn't I hate those who hate You?
>> Shouldn't I despise those who resist You?
²² Yes, I hate them with complete hatred,
>> for Your enemies are my enemies.

²³ Search me, O God, and know my heart;
>> test me and know my thoughts.
²⁴ Point out anything in me that offends You,
>> and lead me along the path of everlasting life.

Proverbs 29

Whoever stubbornly refuses to accept criticism will suddenly be broken beyond repair.

²When the godly are in authority, the people rejoice. But when the wicked are in power, they groan.

³The man who loves wisdom brings joy to his father, but if he hangs around with prostitutes, his wealth is wasted.

⁴A just king gives stability to his nation, but one who demands bribes destroys it.

⁵To flatter people is to lay a trap for their feet.

⁶Evil people are trapped by sin, but the righteous escape, shouting for joy.

⁷The godly know the rights of the poor; the wicked don't care to know.

⁸Mockers can get a whole town agitated, but those who are wise will calm anger.

⁹If a wise person takes a fool to court, there will be ranting and ridicule but no satisfaction.

¹⁰The bloodthirsty hate the honest, but the upright seek out the honest.

¹¹A fool gives full vent to anger, but a wise person quietly holds it back.

¹²If a ruler honors liars, all his advisers will be wicked.

¹³The poor and the oppressor have this in common—the LORD gives light to the eyes of both.

¹⁴A king who is fair to the poor will have a long reign.

¹⁵To discipline and reprimand a child produces wisdom, but a mother is disgraced by an undisciplined child.

¹⁶When the wicked are in authority, sin increases. But the godly will live to see the tyrant's downfall.

¹⁷Discipline your children, and they will give you happiness and peace of mind.

¹⁸When people do not accept divine guidance, they run wild. But whoever obeys the law is happy.

¹⁹For a servant, mere words are not enough—discipline is needed. For the words may be understood, but they are not heeded.

²⁰There is more hope for a fool than for someone who speaks without thinking.

²¹A servant who is pampered from childhood will later become a rebel.

²²A hot-tempered person starts fights and gets into all kinds of sin.

²³Pride ends in humiliation, while humility brings honor.

²⁴If you assist a thief, you are only hurting yourself. You will be punished if you report the crime, but you will be cursed if you don't.

²⁵Fearing people is a dangerous trap, but to trust the LORD means safety.

²⁶Many seek the ruler's favor, but justice comes from the LORD.

²⁷The godly despise the wicked; the wicked despise the godly.

Notes

_____

_____

_____

_____

_____

_____

_____

_____

_____

_____

_____

_____

_____

_____

_____

_____

_____

_____

_____

_____

Psalm 140

For the choir director: A psalm of David.

¹ O LORD, rescue me from evil people.
　　Preserve me from those who are violent,
² those who plot evil in their hearts
　　and stir up trouble all day long.
³ Their tongues sting like a snake;
　　the poison of a viper drips from their lips.　　*Interlude*

⁴ O LORD, keep me out of the hands of the wicked.
　　Preserve me from those who are violent,
　　for they are plotting against me.
⁵ The proud have set a trap to catch me;
　　they have stretched out a net;
　　they have placed traps all along the way.　　*Interlude*

⁶ I said to the LORD, "You are my God!"
　　Listen, O LORD, to my cries for mercy!
⁷ O Sovereign LORD, my strong savior,
　　You protected me on the day of battle.
⁸ LORD, do not give in to their evil desires.
　　Do not let their evil schemes succeed, O God.
　　　　　　　　　　　　　　　　　Interlude

⁹ Let my enemies be destroyed
   by the very evil they have planned for me.
¹⁰ Let burning coals fall down on their heads,
   or throw them into the fire,
   or into deep pits from which they can't escape.
¹¹ Don't let liars prosper here in our land.
   Cause disaster to fall with great force on
       the violent.

¹² But I know the LORD will surely help those they
       persecute;
   He will maintain the rights of the poor.
¹³ Surely the godly are praising Your name,
   for they will live in Your presence.

Psalm 141

A psalm of David.

¹ O LORD, I am calling to You. Please hurry!
   Listen when I cry to You for help!
² Accept my prayer as incense offered to You,
   and my upraised hands as an evening
       offering.

³ Take control of what I say, O LORD,
   and keep my lips sealed.

⁴ Don't let me lust for evil things;
   don't let me participate in acts of
      wickedness.
Don't let me share in the delicacies
   of those who do evil.

⁵ Let the godly strike me!
   It will be a kindness!
If they reprove me, it is soothing medicine.
   Don't let me refuse it.

But I am in constant prayer
   against the wicked and their deeds.
⁶ When their leaders are thrown down from
      a cliff,
   they will listen to my words and find them
      pleasing.
⁷ Even as a farmer breaks up the soil and brings
      up rocks,
   so the bones of the wicked will be scattered
      without a decent burial.

⁸ I look to You for help, O Sovereign LORD.
   You are my refuge; don't let them kill me.
⁹ Keep me out of the traps they have set for me,
   out of the snares of those who do evil.
¹⁰ Let the wicked fall into their own snares,
   but let me escape.

Psalm 142

A psalm of David, regarding his experience in the cave. A prayer.

¹ I cry out to the LORD;
   I plead for the LORD's mercy.
² I pour out my complaints before Him
   and tell Him all my troubles.
³ For I am overwhelmed,
   and You alone know the way I should
      turn.
 Wherever I go,
   my enemies have set traps for me.
⁴ I look for someone to come and help me,
   but no one gives me a passing thought!
 No one will help me;
   no one cares a bit what happens to me.
⁵ Then I pray to You, O LORD.
   I say, "You are my place of refuge.
   You are all I really want in life.
⁶ Hear my cry,
   for I am very low.
 Rescue me from my persecutors,
   for they are too strong for me.
⁷ Bring me out of prison
   so I can thank You.
 The godly will crowd around me,
   for You treat me kindly."

Psalm 143

A psalm of David.

¹ Hear my prayer, O Lord;
   listen to my plea!
   Answer me because You are faithful and righteous.
² Don't bring Your servant to trial!
   Compared to You, no one is perfect.
³ My enemy has chased me.
   He has knocked me to the ground.
   He forces me to live in darkness like those in
      the grave.
⁴ I am losing all hope;
   I am paralyzed with fear.
⁵ I remember the days of old.
   I ponder all Your great works.
   I think about what You have done.
⁶ I reach out for You.
   I thirst for You as parched land thirsts for rain.

Interlude

⁷ Come quickly, Lord, and answer me,
   for my depression deepens.
  Don't turn away from me,
   or I will die.
⁸ Let me hear of Your unfailing love to me in the morning,
   for I am trusting You.

Show me where to walk,
  for I have come to You in prayer.
⁹ Save me from my enemies, LORD;
  I run to You to hide me.
¹⁰ Teach me to do Your will,
  for You are my God.
  May Your gracious Spirit lead me forward
  on a firm footing.
¹¹ For the glory of Your name, O LORD, save me.
  In Your righteousness, bring me out of this distress.
¹² In Your unfailing love, cut off all my enemies
  and destroy all my foes,
  for I am Your servant.

Psalm 144

A psalm of David.

¹ Bless the LORD, who is my rock.
  He gives me strength for war
  and skill for battle.
² He is my loving ally and my fortress,
  my tower of safety, my deliverer.
  He stands before me as a shield, and I take refuge
  in Him.
  He subdues the nations under me.

³ O LORD, what are mortals that You should notice us,
   mere humans that You should care for us?
⁴ For we are like a breath of air;
   our days are like a passing shadow.

⁵ Bend down the heavens, LORD, and come down.
   Touch the mountains so they billow smoke.
⁶ Release Your lightning bolts and scatter Your enemies!
   Release Your arrows and confuse them!
⁷ Reach down from heaven and rescue me;
   deliver me from deep waters,
   from the power of my enemies.
⁸ Their mouths are full of lies;
   they swear to tell the truth, but they lie.

⁹ I will sing a new song to You, O God!
   I will sing Your praises with a ten-stringed harp.
¹⁰ For You grant victory to kings!
   You are the One who rescued Your servant David.
¹¹ Save me from the fatal sword!
   Rescue me from the power of my enemies.
   Their mouths are full of lies;
      they swear to tell the truth, but they lie.

¹² May our sons flourish in their youth
   like well-nurtured plants.
   May our daughters be like graceful pillars,
      carved to beautify a palace.

¹³ May our farms be filled
    with crops of every kind.
  May the flocks in our fields multiply by the
      thousands,
    even tens of thousands,
¹⁴   and may our oxen be loaded down with produce.
  May there be no breached walls, no forced exile,
    no cries of distress in our squares.
¹⁵ Yes, happy are those who have it like this!
    Happy indeed are those whose God is the LORD.

Proverbs 30

The message of Agur son of Jakeh. An oracle.

I am weary, O God; I am weary and worn out, O God. ²I am too ignorant to be human, and I lack common sense. ³I have not mastered human wisdom, nor do I know the Holy One.

⁴Who but God goes up to heaven and comes back down? Who holds the wind in His fists? Who wraps up the oceans in His cloak? Who has created the whole wide world? What is His name—and His Son's name? Tell me if you know!

⁵Every word of God proves true. He defends all who come to Him for protection. ⁶Do not add to His words, or He may rebuke you, and you will be found a liar. ⁷O God, I

beg two favors from You before I die. ⁸First, help me never
to tell a lie. Second, give me neither poverty nor riches!
Give me just enough to satisfy my needs. ⁹For if I grow
rich, I may deny You and say, "Who is the LORD?" And if
I am too poor, I may steal and thus insult God's holy name.

¹⁰Never slander a person to his employer. If you do, the
person will curse you, and you will pay for it.

¹¹Some people curse their father and do not thank their
mother. ¹²They feel pure, but they are filthy and unwashed.
¹³They are proud beyond description and disdainful.
¹⁴They devour the poor with teeth as sharp as swords or
knives. They destroy the needy from the face of the
earth.

¹⁵The leech has two suckers that cry out, "More, more!"
There are three other things—no, four!—that are never
satisfied:
¹⁶ the grave,
  the barren womb,
  the thirsty desert,
  the blazing fire.

¹⁷The eye that mocks a father and despises a mother will
be plucked out by ravens of the valley and eaten by
vultures.

¹⁸There are three things that amaze me—no, four things
I do not understand:

¹⁹ how an eagle glides through the sky,
  how a snake slithers on a rock,
  how a ship navigates the ocean,
  how a man loves a woman.

²⁰Equally amazing is how an adulterous woman can satisfy
her sexual appetite, shrug her shoulders, and then say,
"What's wrong with that?"

  ²¹There are three things that make the earth tremble—
no, four it cannot endure:
²² a slave who becomes a king,
  an overbearing fool who prospers,
²³ a bitter woman who finally gets a husband,
  a servant girl who supplants her mistress.

  ²⁴There are four things on earth that are small but
unusually wise:
²⁵ Ants—they aren't strong,
    but they store up food for the winter.
²⁶ Rock badgers—they aren't powerful,
    but they make their homes among the rocky cliffs.
²⁷ Locusts—they have no king,
    but they march like an army in ranks.
²⁸ Lizards—they are easy to catch,
    but they are found even in kings' palaces.

  ²⁹There are three stately monarchs on the earth—no,
four:

³⁰ the lion, king of animals, who won't turn aside for
  anything,
³¹ the strutting rooster,
  the male goat,
  a king as he leads his army.

³²If you have been a fool by being proud or plotting evil, don't brag about it—cover your mouth with your hand in shame.

³³As the beating of cream yields butter, and a blow to the nose causes bleeding, so anger causes quarrels.

Notes

_____

_____

_____

_____

_____

_____

_____

_____

_____

Psalm 145

A psalm of praise of David.

¹ I will praise You, my God and King,
and bless Your name forever and ever.
² I will bless You every day,
and I will praise You forever.
³ Great is the LORD! He is most worthy of praise!
His greatness is beyond discovery!

⁴ Let each generation tell its children
of Your mighty acts.
⁵ I will meditate on Your majestic, glorious
splendor
and Your wonderful miracles.
⁶ Your awe-inspiring deeds will be on every tongue;
I will proclaim Your greatness.
⁷ Everyone will share the story of Your wonderful
goodness;
they will sing with joy of Your righteousness.

⁸ The LORD is kind and merciful,
slow to get angry, full of unfailing love.

⁹ The LORD is good to everyone.

He showers compassion on all His creation.

¹⁰ All of Your works will thank You, LORD,

and Your faithful followers will bless You.

¹¹ They will talk together about the glory of Your
kingdom;

they will celebrate examples of Your power.

¹² They will tell about Your mighty deeds

and about the majesty and glory of Your reign.

¹³ For Your kingdom is an everlasting kingdom.

You rule generation after generation.

The LORD is faithful in all He says;

He is gracious in all He does.

¹⁴ The LORD helps the fallen

and lifts up those bent beneath their loads.

¹⁵ All eyes look to You for help;

You give them their food as they need it.

¹⁶ When You open Your hand,

You satisfy the hunger and thirst of every
living thing.

¹⁷ The LORD is righteous in everything He does;

He is filled with kindness.

¹⁸ The LORD is close to all who call on Him,

yes, to all who call on Him sincerely.

¹⁹ He fulfills the desires of those who fear Him;

He hears their cries for help and rescues them.

²⁰ The LORD protects all those who love Him,
   but He destroys the wicked.

²¹ I will praise the LORD,
   and everyone on earth will bless His holy name
   forever and forever.

Psalm 146

¹ Praise the LORD!

Praise the LORD, I tell myself.
² I will praise the LORD as long as I live.
   I will sing praises to my God even with my dying
   breath.

³ Don't put your confidence in powerful people;
   there is no help for you there.
⁴ When their breathing stops, they return to the
   earth,
   and in a moment all their plans come to an end.
⁵ But happy are those who have the God of Israel
   as their helper,
   whose hope is in the LORD their God.
⁶ He is the One who made heaven and earth,
   the sea, and everything in them.

He is the One who keeps every promise forever,
7   who gives justice to the oppressed
    and food to the hungry.
The LORD frees the prisoners.
8   The LORD opens the eyes of the blind.
The LORD lifts the burdens of those bent beneath their
        loads.
    The LORD loves the righteous.
9 The LORD protects the foreigners among us.
    He cares for the orphans and widows,
    but He frustrates the plans of the wicked.

10 The LORD will reign forever.
    O Jerusalem, your God is King in every generation!

Praise the LORD!

Psalm 147

1 Praise the LORD!

How good it is to sing praises to our God!
    How delightful and how right!
2 The LORD is rebuilding Jerusalem
    and bringing the exiles back to Israel.
3 He heals the brokenhearted,
    binding up their wounds.

⁴ He counts the stars
    and calls them all by name.
⁵ How great is our Lord! His power is absolute!
    His understanding is beyond comprehension!
⁶ The LORD supports the humble,
    but He brings the wicked down into the dust.

⁷ Sing out your thanks to the LORD;
    sing praises to our God, accompanied by harps.
⁸ He covers the heavens with clouds,
    provides rain for the earth,
    and makes the green grass grow in mountain
        pastures.
⁹ He feeds the wild animals,
    and the young ravens cry to Him for food.
¹⁰ The strength of a horse does not impress Him;
    how puny in His sight is the strength of a man.
¹¹ Rather, the LORD's delight is in those who honor Him,
    those who put their hope in His unfailing love.

¹² Praise the LORD, O Jerusalem!
    Praise your God, O Zion!
¹³ For He has fortified the bars of your gates
    and blessed your children within you.
¹⁴ He sends peace across your nation
    and satisfies you with plenty of the finest wheat.
¹⁵ He sends His orders to the world—
    how swiftly His word flies!

¹⁶ He sends the snow like white wool;
>   he scatters frost upon the ground like
>   ashes.
¹⁷ He hurls the hail like stones.
>   Who can stand against His freezing cold?
¹⁸ Then, at His command, it all melts.
>   He sends His winds, and the ice thaws.

¹⁹ He has revealed His words to Jacob,
>   His principles and laws to Israel.
²⁰ He has not done this with any other nation;
>   they do not know His laws.

Praise the LORD!

Psalm 148

¹ Praise the LORD!

Praise the LORD from the heavens!
>   Praise Him from the skies!
² Praise Him, all His angels!
>   Praise Him, all the armies of heaven!
³ Praise Him, sun and moon!
>   Praise Him, all you twinkling stars!
⁴ Praise Him, skies above!
>   Praise Him, vapors high above the clouds!

⁵ Let every created thing give praise to the LORD,
    for He issued His command, and they came
       into being.
⁶ He established them forever and forever.
    His orders will never be revoked.

⁷ Praise the LORD from the earth,
    you creatures of the ocean depths,
⁸ fire and hail, snow and storm,
    wind and weather that obey Him,
⁹ mountains and all hills,
    fruit trees and all cedars,
¹⁰ wild animals and all livestock,
    reptiles and birds,
¹¹ kings of the earth and all people,
    rulers and judges of the earth,
¹² young men and maidens,
    old men and children.
¹³ Let them all praise the name of the LORD.
    For His name is very great;
    His glory towers over the earth and
       heaven!
¹⁴ He has made His people strong,
    honoring His godly ones—
    the people of Israel who are close to Him.

    Praise the LORD!

Psalm 149

¹ Praise the LORD!

Sing to the LORD a new song.
  Sing His praises in the assembly of the
    faithful.
² O Israel, rejoice in your Maker.
  O people of Jerusalem, exult in your
    King.
³ Praise His name with dancing,
  accompanied by tambourine and harp.
⁴ For the LORD delights in His people;
  He crowns the humble with salvation.
⁵ Let the faithful rejoice in this honor.
  Let them sing for joy as they lie on
    their beds.
⁶ Let the praises of God be in their mouths,
  and a sharp sword in their hands—
⁷ to execute vengeance on the nations
  and punishment on the peoples,
⁸ to bind their kings with shackles
  and their leaders with iron chains,
⁹ to execute the judgment written against
    them.
  This is the glory of His faithful ones.

Praise the LORD!

Psalm 150

¹ Praise the LORD!

Praise God in His heavenly dwelling;
  praise Him in His mighty heaven!
² Praise Him for His mighty works;
  praise His unequaled greatness!
³ Praise Him with a blast of the trumpet;
  praise Him with the lyre and harp!
⁴ Praise Him with the tambourine and dancing;
  praise Him with stringed instruments and flutes!
⁵ Praise Him with a clash of cymbals;
  praise Him with loud clanging cymbals.
⁶ Let everything that lives sing praises to the LORD!

Praise the LORD!

Proverbs 31

These are the sayings of King Lemuel, an oracle that his
mother taught him.

²O my son, O son of my womb, O son of my promises,
³do not spend your strength on women, on those who ruin
kings.

⁴And it is not for kings, O Lemuel, to guzzle wine.

Rulers should not crave liquor. ⁵For if they drink, they may forget their duties and be unable to give justice to those who are oppressed. ⁶Liquor is for the dying, and wine for those in deep depression. ⁷Let them drink to forget their poverty and remember their troubles no more.

⁸Speak up for those who cannot speak for themselves; ensure justice for those who are perishing. ⁹Yes, speak up for the poor and helpless, and see that they get justice.

¹⁰Who can find a virtuous and capable wife? She is worth more than precious rubies. ¹¹Her husband can trust her, and she will greatly enrich his life. ¹²She will not hinder him but help him all her life.

¹³She finds wool and flax and busily spins it. ¹⁴She is like a merchant's ship; she brings her food from afar. ¹⁵She gets up before dawn to prepare breakfast for her household and plan the day's work for her servant girls. ¹⁶She goes out to inspect a field and buys it; with her earnings she plants a vineyard.

¹⁷She is energetic and strong, a hard worker. ¹⁸She watches for bargains; her lights burn late into the night. ¹⁹Her hands are busy spinning thread, her fingers twisting fiber.

²⁰She extends a helping hand to the poor and opens her arms to the needy.

²¹She has no fear of winter for her household because all of them have warm clothes. ²²She quilts her own bedspreads. She dresses like royalty in gowns of finest cloth.

²³Her husband is well known, for he sits in the council meeting with the other civic leaders.

²⁴She makes belted linen garments and sashes to sell to the merchants.

²⁵She is clothed with strength and dignity, and she laughs with no fear of the future. ²⁶When she speaks, her words are wise, and kindness is the rule when she gives instructions. ²⁷She carefully watches all that goes on in her household and does not have to bear the consequences of laziness.

²⁸Her children stand and bless her. Her husband praises her: ²⁹"There are many virtuous and capable women in the world, but you surpass them all!"

³⁰Charm is deceptive, and beauty does not last; but a woman who fears the LORD will be greatly praised. ³¹Reward her for all she has done. Let her deeds publicly declare her praise.

Notes

_____

_____

_____

_____

_____

_____

_____

_____

_____

_____

_____

_____

_____

_____

_____

_____

_____

Interpretive Note

Psalms

When the eleven disciples were gathered behind locked doors on the night of Christ's resurrection, we are told that they were greatly disturbed and fearful. Then the Lord entered the room and said to them, "Peace be with you" (Luke 24:36). What He brought to the disciples He can bring to the mind and heart of any individual who will let Him in.

Jesus began His discourse to the disciples by saying, "Why are you frightened? . . . Look at my hands. Look at my feet. You can see that it's really me. Touch me and make sure that I am not a ghost, because ghosts don't have bodies, as you see that I do!" Then he turned to them and said, "Do you have anything here to eat?" Jesus concluded by saying, "When I was with you before, I told you that everything written about me by Moses and the prophets and in the Psalms must all come true." And Luke adds: "Then he opened their minds to understand these many Scriptures" (24:38-45).

Thus it is on the authority of the Lord Jesus Christ Himself that we are to find Christ in the Psalms. No one can properly understand the Cross or fathom why Jesus endured its agony without having studied the Psalms. For example, when we read Luke 24, we see its relationship to Psalm 1. The first three verses of Psalm 1 convey that the one who does not follow the advice of the wicked is blessed and happy.

"Oh, the joys of those who do not follow the advice of the wicked, . . . or join in with scoffers. But they delight in doing everything the LORD wants; day and night they think about his law. They are like trees planted along the riverbank, bearing fruit each season without fail. Their leaves never wither, and in all they do, they prosper."

The only one who could experience this completely is the Lord Jesus Christ, for He is the only one who never walked in the counsel of the ungodly.

While the first three verses of Psalm 1 speak particularly of Christ, the one who believes in Christ can also describe his or her position with the Lord in terms of these verses. Certainly there is no true and lasting happiness in this world today apart from the Blessed One, that is to say, apart from the Lord Jesus Christ.

Proverbs

Of all inspired thoughts in the book of Proverbs, the key statement is found in chapter 3, verses 13-14: "Happy is the person who finds wisdom and gains understanding. For the profit of wisdom is better than silver, and her wages are better than gold." When we read God's Word, it is God speaking to people. When Christians pray, it is people speaking to God.

In the Psalms, Christians are found on their knees. In the book of Proverbs, Christians are found on their feet doing things. The Psalms are for devotion; the Proverbs are for the Christian's walk and warfare. The Proverbs are for the business-person, for the layperson, for young people in their everyday walk and life, and for the church leader.

In the opening verse of the book of Proverbs, we read the superscription, "These are the proverbs of Solomon, David's son, king of Israel." We are told that what follows is given for our wisdom and instruction. Solomon was a great scientist and philosopher. He was also the architect of one of the wonders of the ancient world, the temple in Jerusalem. He was also a king. In 1 Kings 4:29, we read that "God gave Solomon great wisdom and understanding, and knowledge too vast to be measured."

Solomon gathered sayings given by the Holy Spirit, arranged them in an orderly fashion, and preserved them for us and our daily instruction.

In the first ten chapters of Proverbs, we find counsel for young people. The second ten provide counsel for people in all stages of life. The next chapters, 21–30, are counsel for kings and rulers, and the book closes with chapter 31, a beautiful description of women's rights.

May you find much joy and strength in your reading, and may you find, as Solomon did, that "Timely advice is as lovely as golden apples in a silver basket" (Proverbs 25:11).

G. M. W.

Where to Find Help in the Psalms

Read these chapters when you:

Feel troubled *17, 20, 23, 27, 28, 40, 43, 54, 57, 62, 63, 64, 67, 86*

Have sinned *56, 59, 69, 70, 102, 140, 141, 142, 143*

Feel "cornered" *36, 68*

Feel things have "gone sour" *42*

Feel like complaining *39*

Feel envious of people *73*

Feel your friends have turned against you *35, 41, 55*

Need assurance *3*

Are angry with someone *133*

Have sinned *32, 51, 79, 80, 106, 130*

Need help *38, 83*

Are facing important decisions *25, 26, 91*

Are troubled by godlessness in the world *2, 9, 46, 52, 75, 76*

Need encouragement as a senior citizen *71*

Feel timid about sharing your faith *67*

Have responsibility in governing others *21, 72, 82, 94*

Find it difficult to be thankful *66*

Need to get your mind off yourself and praise God *92, 96, 97, 98, 100, 117, 136, 138, 139, 145, 147, 148, 150*

These Psalms
Will Remind You That:

God and one are a majority *18*
God is worth trusting *4, 29, 33, 34, 65, 99, 118*
God loves His own *8, 31, 81, 91, 105, 106, 111, 121, 149*
God hears our prayers *103, 108, 116*
God is alive *8, 14, 84, 115*
God is in control of history *24, 45, 47, 87, 99, 110, 124, 135*
God is incomparable *19, 65, 107, 113, 114, 146*
God is the source of life *104*
God's words are most important *119*
Godly living is great living *1, 15, 16, 112, 127, 128*
Godly living benefits a nation *78, 144*
Our Creator can best guide our lives *25, 37*
Those who govern should honor God *21*
We should pray for the Jews *44, 48, 74, 122, 126, 129, 132*
Jesus also suffered *22*
We should keep a Godly perspective in life *90, 93*
No one fools God *5, 10, 11, 12, 50, 53*
Humans alone are nothing *2, 9, 49, 124, 131*
We are sinful *32*

*Highlights in Proverbs
on the Subjects of:*

Children, raising of *13:24; 14:26; 19:18; 22:6; 23:13-14; 29:15, 17*

Counsel *10:20-21, 31; 12:1, 15, 26; 13:1, 10, 14, 18; 14:7, 15; 15:5, 7, 23, 31-32; 18:2, 13, 15, 20; 19:2, 20; 20:5, 18; 23:12, 23; 25:11; 28:13; 29:1*

Friendliness *12:25; 16:28; 17:9, 17; 18:24; 27:10, 19*

Goals in life *3:21-26*

Government *8:14-16; 11:14; 14:35; 16:10, 12; 17:23; 18:5; 20:8, 26, 28; 22:8; 28:2, 15-16; 29:2, 4, 12, 14, 16*

Health *3:7-8; 4:21-22; 14:27, 30; 15:4, 15, 30; 16:24; 17:22; 19:23*

Immorality *2:16-19; 4:23-27; 5:1-23; 6:24-35; 7:1-27; 9:13-18; 22:14; 23:26-28; 24:8; 30:20*

Integrity *3:27-28; 11:1, 3, 6; 12:13, 17, 22; 13:5; 14:25; 15:3; 16:2, 11; 17:15; 19:5, 9, 28; 20:10, 21, 23; 21:2-3; 30:10*

Justice *3:33; 10:30; 11:19, 21, 31; 12:7, 19; 13:23; 14:11, 19, 32; 22:7-8; 24:11-12, 19-20; 28:5; 29:17, 26*

Keys to life *3:1-6; 8:13; 22:17-19*

Marriage *11:29; 12:4; 14:1; 18:22; 19:14; 21:9, 19; 27:15-16; 31:10-31*

Money-lending *6:1-5; 11:15; 17:18; 20:16; 22:26-27; 27:13*

Parents, respect for *6:20-23; 10:1; 15:20; 17:25; 19:26; 20:20; 23:15-16, 22, 24-25; 27:11; 29:3*

STEPS TO PEACE WITH GOD

1. RECOGNIZE GOD'S PLAN—PEACE AND LIFE

The message you have read in this book stresses that God loves you and wants you to experience His peace and life.

The BIBLE says . . . *"For God loved the world so much that He gave His only Son, so that everyone who believes in Him may not die but have eternal life." John 3:16*

2. REALIZE OUR PROBLEM—SEPARATION

People choose to disobey God and go their own way. This results in separation from God.

The BIBLE says . . . *"Everyone has sinned and is far away from God's saving presence." Romans 3:23*

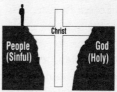

3. RESPOND TO GOD'S REMEDY—CROSS OF CHRIST

God sent His Son to bridge the gap. Christ did this by paying the penalty of our sins when He died on the cross and rose from the grave.

The BIBLE says . . . *"But God has shown us how much He loves us—it was while we were still sinners that Christ died for us!" Romans 5:8*

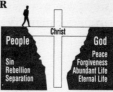

4. RECEIVE GOD'S SON—LORD AND SAVIOR

You cross the bridge into God's family when you ask Christ to come into your life.

The BIBLE says . . . *"Some, however, did receive Him and believed in Him; so He gave them the right to become God's children." John 1:12*

THE INVITATION IS TO:
REPENT (turn from your sins) and by faith RECEIVE Jesus Christ into your heart and life and follow Him in obedience as your Lord and Savior.

PRAYER OF COMMITMENT
"Lord Jesus, I know I am a sinner. I believe You died for my sins. Right now, I turn from my sins and open the door of my heart and life. I receive You as my personal Lord and Savior. Thank You for saving me now. Amen."

If you want further help in the decision you have made, write to:
Billy Graham Evangelistic Association, P.O. Box 779, Minneapolis, MN 55440-0779

If you are committing your life to Christ, please let us know! We would like to send you Bible study materials and a complimentary six-month subscription to *Decision* magazine to help you grow in your faith.

The Billy Graham Evangelistic Association exists to support the evangelistic ministry and calling of Billy Graham to take the message of Christ to all we can by every prudent means available to us.

Our desire is to introduce as many as we can to the person of Jesus Christ, so that they might experience His love and forgiveness.

Your prayers are the most important way to support us in this ministry. We are grateful for the dedicated prayer support we receive. We are also grateful for those that support us with contributions.

Giving can be a rewarding experience for you and for us at the Billy Graham Evangelistic Association (BGEA). Your gift gives you the satisfaction of supporting an organization that is actively involved in evangelism. Also, it is encouraging to us because part of our ministry is devoted to helping people like you discover and enjoy the stewardship of giving wisely and effectively.

Billy Graham Evangelistic Association
P.O. Box 779
Minneapolis, Minnesota 55440-0779
www.billygraham.org

Billy Graham Evangelistic Association of Canada
P.O. Box 841, Stn Main
Winnipeg, Manitoba R3C 2R3
www.billygraham.ca

Toll free: 1-877-247-2426